A South African woman triumphs over numerous adversities, thanks largely to the power of her faith. In her debut, Bryant details a number of hardships that she and her husband faced while running a photographic studio in Port Shepstone, South Africa, including devaluation of the local currency, an economic depression, and drought. "I could not fathom the turn of events when I witnessed our frightening, declining available cash balance," she writes. Added into the mix was the author's often precarious health, due to complications from a serious accident she suffered as a child.

Bryant writes that at times she seemed to reach her breaking point. Through it all, however, she says that she found two main sources of respite: horses, and her faith in God. A lifelong equestrian, she provides many details about horses she has known: "Cheeko was perfect. He was a fourteen one hand dun gelding." Her faith, meanwhile, is showcased in a variety of ways, from biblical quotes to an ocean baptism and more. In one particularly memorable scene, the author conquers the "spirit of unbelief" within herself: "Eventually I coughed, and with a loud groaning the foreign body was spewed out with force." Loyal to her husband even in the most difficult times, the author admits to occasional strife with other family members over religious issues: "This added to my pain, for the believer's strong emotion is that we want our loved ones to *know and understand* that they might inherit eternal life." Readers intrigued by unusual, faith-based events will encounter many throughout this book, such as a scene in which Bryant says that an "ear-shattering screech flashed from my mouth, and appeared to hit the ceiling of the room, as an explosion within the room would do."

Although nonbelievers are unlikely to be swayed by any of these happenings, readers of a similar mindset will find much to relish here. The book ably encompasses both the miraculous and the commonplace, and, on the whole, does a good job of explaining one woman's de~~ ~~~~~~~d beliefs and the events in her life that caused them.

An often intriguing religious memoir.

Kirkus Indie, Kirkus Media LLC, 6411 Burleson Rd., Austin, TX 78744
indie@kirkusreviews.com

THE HORSE AND HIS RIDER

THE HORSE AND HIS RIDER

REVEALED IN SPIRITUAL WARFARE AND DELIVERANCE

Charmazelle Bryant

PARTRIDGE

A Penguin Random House Company

To order additional copies of this book, contact
Toll Free 0800 990 914 (South Africa)
+44 20 3014 3997 (outside South Africa)
orders.africa@partridgepublishing.com

www.partridgepublishing.com/africa

This book is dedicated to:

- *Those who need a miracle*
- *Those who will accept my testimony*
- *and, Those who will ride on white horses in the army of the Lord*

Note I: **Scripture references**

God's written word forms so dynamic a part of this testimony that, in parts it was thought better not to interrupt the flow with specific citations for each Bible quotation. Where the numerals of chapter and verse were given by the Spirit, these are mentioned as the Spirit spoke. The bibles versions used in the citations of texts in this book are: Authorised King James, New King James, New American Standard, and New International. All bible citations are from the New King James Version, unless otherwise mentioned.

Note II: **Names**

This book is a testimony of victory in the spirit, thanks to Jesus, in whose Name there is no variableness, nor shadow of turning. His Name remains the same when mentioned in this text. The events are true; the circumstances are true; and the miracles of God are true. The names that have been changed are the names of all the people, who came into my life, helped, hindered and ministered to me during the time frame here recorded.

INTRODUCTION

Horses have evoked mystique, aroused passion, inspired art, elevated status, and empowered speed, mobility and strength throughout history and folklore. Valiant knights of old rode horses into battle; and none could challenge the mighty horse and his rider. This book brings together overcoming the mighty and maintaining the love and passion for the horse as a prized creation of nature. Horses are mentioned in one hundred and eighty eight bible verses, symbolising types and shadows of spiritual warfare, and singular triumphs in the spirit world.

Devaluation of the South African Rand on the international market, combined with global economic depression, and drought on the Natal South Coast were factors that I, Charmazelle, was not aware of. I could not fathom the turn of events when I witnessed our frightening, declining available cash balance…. My husband, Tim Bryant and I ran a family business – a photographic studio and picture framing shop, in the small coastal town of Port Shepstone. The shock of dark elements creeping in upon us, unseen from the economic ignominy, made me particularly protective of our three young children, alias the lioness protecting her cubs.

The emotional stress of the threatened loss of our small holding during a period of just over half a year was a real and devastating factor. The property was particularly sentimental: some years before the impending crash, Tim and I had purchased a windy hilltop – twenty acres of bare veld, with a distant sea view. We had cut a road into the property, planted trees for windbreaks, hoed out thick, indigenous grass to plant lawns, and etched a garden around the small cottage that we built. I can still see our African assistant handing me bricks, and feel the weight of the wet mortar on my trowel. I was seven months pregnant with my first child when I built in the gables on a high scaffold.

In our desperate attempt to hold onto our property which had been mortgaged to finance our business, we turned to God. We were rewarded by incredible miracles of provision; and, through it all, our lives were steered in a direction that we had not contemplated; but also, through it all, a way was opened for my children and I to hold onto our precious horses …..

CONTENTS

Bible citations to chapters that have been named from scripture extracts are as follows:

Chapter 1 Matthew 10:14
Chapter 5 Jeremiah 30:12
Chapter 10 Matthew 26:12 NIV
Chapter 11 Isaiah 66:9
Chapter 12 Isaiah 52:1
Chapter 14 Psalm 51:17
Chapter 15 Hebrews 4:12
Chapter 16 Jeremiah 31:33
Chapter 17 John 16:33
Chapter 19 Revelation 19:14 Authorised KJV
Chapter 20 Jeremiah 30:17

ONE

SHAKE OFF THE DUST FROM YOUR FEET

The tempo of the work was fast that Monday morning, like a heartbeat too rapid for comfort. The time was approximately ten o'clock. The first day of the working week was always the busiest in the darkroom, because not only had the Friday and Saturday routine work to be processed, but weekend weddings, functions or sporting events inevitably added to the work-load.

Photographic processing was in full swing. Exposed paper lay in a tray of developer, prints were in the fixing solution, tap water bubbled over prints in the washer. The production machine was in gear. The interlocking teeth caused the mechanism to grind slowly forward. I knew that I had to force the pace: identity and licence photographs were always deadline material; portrait enlargement's had to be ready for 'granny's birthday'; advertising photographs had to be available for the local newspaper before they went to print on Tuesday morning. Work tumbled upon work!

It was at this time, when I was drowning in the myriad tasks the business required of me, that I reached for a bible that was lying on the work bench next to one of the enlargers. The room was lit only by a dim glow from the red safe-light. It occurred to me that I had never asked the Lord for

a word before (not long ago I did not even know that one could do that!)
Therefore I asked in a childlike, straightforward manner. As I was phrasing
the request, "Lord, please give me a word", the answer came as a distinct
thought picture:

"Matthew chapter ten, verse fourteen."

Deftly I placed any unexposed paper that was lying around into light-tight
containers, and then quickly brought the semi-processed prints through the
chemicals. I could then turn on the main light, and I pulled a high stool
closer to the work bench. There I perched in the silence of the darkroom,
conscious of loneliness, separation, and the isolation of my surroundings.
Placing the bible between the enlarger and a tray of chemical, I opened it
to search for the scripture.

> "And when you go into a household, greet it. If the house is
> worthy, let your peace come upon it. But if it is not worthy,
> let your peace return to you. And whoever will not receive
> you, nor hear your words, when you depart from that house
> or city, shake off the dust of your feet"
>
> Matthew 10:12-14

Those last seven words stood out significantly. But this seemed ridiculous!
Why? Obviously there was some mistake. I hadn't heard aright. It was my
imagination, my own thoughts, just a co-incidence that led me to that
scripture. There were more reasons than I could count to suggest that this
scripture was, at the time, irrelevant to my circumstances. Possibly I had not
prayed properly, when asking for a word. Possibly my request should have
been more fervent, or more formally worded!

Then I had to analyse why I was embarking on this strange mission. Perhaps
it was not actually possible to ask God for a word. Surely it was a ridiculous
exercise! Why was I asking for a word, anyway?

Our friend and mentor, Rob Knight, who had been at the waterside two years previously, when my husband, Timothy, and I were baptized in the sea; who had laid hands on us as we knelt on the beach sands, and prayed until we received the baptism in the Spirit and spoke with new tongues, had said to me yesterday:

"Get a word from the Lord about baptism."

Surely it was a quest in vain. Either the Lord did not hear, or did not answer my question.

Disappointment made me feel despondent. I needed to get out of the darkroom, if for no other reason than to make a cup of tea. With this in mind I carefully closed the boxes of different sized photographic paper, and ensured that they were light tight; then with a glance I scanned the room now bathed in soft, red light and checked that all was in order for me to open the door.

The sunlight was beautiful in the garden! It took a while for my eyes to adjust to the natural light. Lawns and shrubs and trees shone in shades of emerald, lime, and bright green in the sunlight, contrasting beautifully with the olive greens of the shadows. Our trees were now tall enough to shade a person standing beneath them! It was a delight to see the trees and shrubs that my husband, Tim and I had planted, flourishing on our wind blown hilltop. Stepping away from the house, downhill on the north side, I surveyed our place as it was now was with addition of a new wing to accommodate the darkroom, which enabled us to work at night from home. I looked up at the structure with pride! The three large, arches, finished in white painted Spanish plaster, topped with the characteristic terra cotta clay tiles etched a stately façade against a cloudless, cerulean sky......... Eventually I had the Spanish arches I dreamed of!

To digress here, our friend, Rob Knight, who now lived by faith, had been in an advisory position in building research at a national institution.

When Tim and I had told him we planned to add a wing to our house, and complete the north facing stoep with Spanish arches, he had said at the time, that he would come and show me how to construct the arches. However, as we lived far apart, we did not see him for some time. Masonry, building and plastering were my hobby. I could create when I had a trowel in my hand. I loved the feel of wet, freshly mixed cement beneath the steel blade! It was two months after the birth of my third child when I was up on a scaffold figuring out how to build an arch. I remember seeing an old, scrap tractor tire on a neighbour's property in the far distance; and that became the basis of the formwork for the reinforcing.

Rob was surprised when he visited us: "You've done it already!"

I seem to remember I just smiled.

Standing under a Macadamia nut tree in the lower part of the garden, near our front gate, I looked up to check if there were nuts forming. Nothing there: I was told it took many years. I did my best to believe that the day would come.........

From the front gate below the house, our driveway was cut in conical formation, which wound gradually round our lofty hilltop, to reduce the incline. By stepping down a small embankment, I reached the gate to our land, then walked up the driveway, now an avenue, which wound from the north side to the back door on the south side.

Before entering the house, I paused to look down, past the horse stables, to the valley on the south side. There was a vista of veld interspersed with bush, and an overgrown banana plantation on very steep land. Far below there was a water hole. That water hole was purported to be a permanent spring by the estate agent that sold the property to us some ten years previously. However, the cost of getting power to that water hole, which was situated about 200 metres from our house, was far too high to be considered. Moreover, the water hole was alongside the district road that ran through the bottom of our property, southwards, toward the low level bridge over the Umzimkulu River, and on to the town of Port Shepstone. This road was our shortest route to the town.. In Africa, a pump alongside a district road was vulnerable beyond words. However, the main deterrent was the quality of the little bit of muddy water. There was no municipal water connection to the property, and we had always survived by storing rain water in our tanks. Looking down at that land towards that valley, I tried to visualize the national freeway that would slice off about a third of our twenty acres. The plans for this freeway were on the drawing board. How long would it be? How much would they pay us out? But the big question was: could we last until then?

I entered the house to make the tea I was wanting.

It was early August. Despite the clear, radiant sunshine outside, the chill of winter could still be felt indoors. I warmed both hands on my cup, and sipped the hot, welcome liquid, thinking about the new situation of having the darkroom at home. For several years Tim and I had owned and run two photographic studios in two adjacent South Coast towns, Port Shepstone and Margate. Our small holding was ten kilometres north of Port Shepstone, and much further from Margate which was about another fifteen kilometres to the south. There was a heyday, and there were good years; and our hearts were full of hope and ambition. We basked in the belief that times would get better and better. However, good years go past and take the essence of their goodness with them, but one does not forget those times, and strives constantly to recreate them; the dream does not fade, because the circumstances do not match the dream. The lean years creep in; slither in silently; arrive unexpectedly. Suddenly one has to cope with a different scenario. Could it be the implementation of a national fiscal policy that was taking the bread off the tables of the hungry? If, indeed it was, neither Tim nor I understood what was happening.

We found ourselves in a position where our turnover was insufficient to yield enough cash flow to meet the overheads, keep the vehicles running, feed the family, and keep up payments to our trade creditors. This was the stressful situation that closed in around us. All we could see our way clear to doing was to work harder and cut costs. Both businesses were running at a loss. We realized that we had to reduce diversification, concentrate our efforts on one studio and retail outlet, and reduce staff costs by working at night. To implement this plan, we gave our Margate business, which housed the processing darkroom, away to a fellow Christian for the price of its trade creditors, and built a darkroom at home.........

The tea was finished. The darkroom was calling.

I settled in, adjusting my eyes to the faint red light in the darkness and got the work going. After a while, the fact that I did not get a satisfactory word from the Lord, again began to worry me. I *had* to ask again! Accordingly I adjusted the materials that had to be light proof, and switched on a light by which I could read.

I tried to compose a more eloquently worded prayer. After all, I was approaching Almighty God, creator of heaven and of earth. My invocation had to be correct! As I began to choose the proper words, my prayer was curtailed by the answer:

"Luke nine, verse five."

I tucked my legs more firmly under the bar stool and repositioned my feet on the cross piece that stabilised it, while I paged through the gospels to find the second scripture. When I found the chapter and verse, I had to focus my eyes again and again to justify the surprise I felt! The scripture read:

> "And whoever will not receive you, when you go out of that **city**, *shake off the dust from your feet,* as a testimony against them."

Luke 9:5 (Italics mine)

My immediate reaction was to attribute this to co-incidence. However, I *knew* that this was not co-incidence. I knew that God knew that I had had no idea that those similar scriptures were located in any particular chapter and verse. What was God saying to me? It was scary. Thoughts of hidden areas and secret passions in my life came to mind, while I sat there with bent knees and arched back – a solitary figure on a tall bar stool, dwarfed by the sombre heads of photographic enlargers.

TWO

THE ACCIDENT

I was a little girl, a butterfly flitting from flower to flower, tasting the nectar, singing a happy song, being a child – exuberant, active, happy and secure! That was the picture one day, the next there was only the still, unseen, dark, unfathomable, silent word of unconsciousness. Merciful, merciful unconsciousness.........

What does an eight year old know about the words trauma, comatose, paralysis and brain damage; and, having coped with the emotional and psychological impact of these concepts, go on to grasp matters such as permanent disability, negligence, liability, and judgements of the Supreme Court?

* * *

My two younger cousins and I had been let loose on the side of a tar road, about a hundred metres before a bridge. The bridge spanned the Vaal river on the main road that linked the two towns of Vereeniging and Parys. On the far side of the bridge the road rose steeply to disappear over a rocky "kopje".

We scampered toward the bridge, far ahead of the two accompanying adults. Our steps were quickened by eagerness and enthusiasm, as we were going to have a picnic! We children took in the scene on the left of the bridge, and then my cousins ran across to look at the scene on the right. I lingered on the left side, then looked back down the road to check for oncoming cars. I saw my aunt's car away in the distance on the downside of the bridge, then I looked up the road towards the stony hill above the bridge. There were no cars in sight. As the others returned from the right hand side, I ran across towards it, not wanting to miss a thing. Once there, on the far side, I stood on tip-toe, leaned over, and gripped the concrete parapet with both arms, momentarily holding my body against the cold concrete so that I could see the exciting sights over the wall; and I formed a quick, clear mental image of the expanse of reeds swaying in the muddy, swirling waters far below before I dashed back to join the others on the left side.........

* * *

Consciousness came two to three weeks after "my accident", but it wasn't all there at once; it came in lapses – confused, painful lapses. I could only relate to my circumstances by the things my mother said. She was the only contact with the real world.

The first mental picture I had on regaining consciousness was of the mass of reeds swirling in the muddy waters below; and I could feel the cold, hard concrete of the parapet beneath my hands and against my body. Then I lapsed back into that other world.

When awakening at later moment, again I caught the strains of my mother's voice vaguely disrupt my spectrum of darkness: "The hospital couldn't handle the case." (The hospital that was closest to the Vaal bridge was a poorly equipped, inadequate institution in a little town that was no more than a village in the year 1950) "When Dr. Vincent first saw her, he said they should put a sheet over her because she won't make it."

And then, once more, as my eyes flickered momentarily open, out of the darkness of the deep sleep, I heard the words: "Oh, my Darling Charmazelle, you are awake! They said you would never wake up."

Again after an unknown period of unconsciousness "You talked so much in your sleep. You would say 'fifteen million years ago', and then 'five minutes ago'." Who can fathom the turmoil of disorientation during such trauma?

Other facts were gleaned, not necessarily in chronological order, of happenings in the short moments of awakening. Sometimes, my Mother spoke to me; sometimes I heard her telling others:

"They said she would have brain damage, as a result of the head injuries. That was the greatest fear, and the reason why Dr. Vincent was of the opinion that it would be better if she slept on.......... But she wakes up from time to time, and you can see from the expression in her eyes that there is no brain damage.

"The imprint of her upper body could be seen in the metal of the car. The bumper hit her right leg. She was flung 75 feet, in a parabola, up into the air, and down toward the river. Her body skidded down the steep gravel embankment, landing a metre or two above the water line. Her fall was broken by a tuft of grass.

"The entire right side of her body and face were lacerated from the steep, stony river bank that she landed on and slid down. She came down head first, and there was a huge piece of flesh, cut from the eyebrow to the hair line, that was hanging loose. The wound was crudely stitched, pulling her eyebrow up over her forehead.

"The right leg had a compound fracture – both tibia and fibula were broken. The tibia was protruding at right angles to the leg. My sister said she had a terrible time carrying Charmazelle in the car to the hospital with that broken leg. Doctor Vincent placed the right leg in plaster without setting the bone. Her life was too much in the balance for her to have undergone the procedure of having the bones properly set.

"The knee of her left leg was badly lacerated from the onslaught of the car. Dr Vincent bandaged the leg just below the knee with a tourniquet to prevent water on the knee. The tourniquet was supposed to be left on for two hours, but because they were only worried about keeping her alive, they forgot it.........

"To assist the hospital with their inadequate staff and facilities, a qualified nursing sister was brought from Johannesburg to give her special care. Dr Vincent instructed the sister to keep her warm. She made a hot water bottle – filled it with boiling water! The right leg was in plaster so she put it on the left foot, while the tourniquet was on!

"They found the damage 48 hours after the tourniquet was put on! When they took that bandage off, the flesh below her knee peeled off with it! The leg had turned blue, *the nerves were severed from the knee down, and the foot had a third degree burn.* It was like a piece of red meat!"

I remember that I had drawn the lower leg up towards my body. The knee remained bent at an acute angle for months, and I must have screamed if anyone tried to touch or straighten the leg. As a result of the paralysis, ankylosis set in, which meant that the ankle was set in an immovable position, turned inward. With the contraction of muscles and tendons, the knee and ankle were locked and the toes were contracted, bent and clawed.

It was to be five years before I underwent the last in a series of operations to straighten the leg sufficiently to walk on, without crutches or irons.

My mother and father took me home from the country hospital as soon as I was able to travel. Our home was situated on the far side of Johannesburg; and the distance had made their visits to the Vereeniging hospital difficult. For a few days, I was made as comfortable as possible in the house I had known since early childhood. Then one day my parents told me that they were taking me back to a hospital.

I pleaded, "I don't want to go to a hospital."

My mother said, "But it is a *children's* hospital!"

*   *   *

The advice was given to them by a specialist doctor called in for consultation by their Johannesburg family doctor.

"Her right leg should be set properly so as to avoid problems later. Hospitalisation is also advisable, taking into consideration that observation is necessary because of the nature of the multiple injuries."

Could my parents have known how great a mistake they were making by taking this advice?

Certainly no expert in clinical psychology was consulted. Did the medical experts not consider it more advisable to let me recover from the shock and trauma in a tranquil home atmosphere? The orthopaedics looked merely at the mechanical issues of a broken leg that needed to be set, and other factors pertaining to my injuries, which, alas, were grossly misjudged. They obviously did not weigh the factors of a familiar, caring home environment against the cruel, lonely isolation of a foreign ward. I needed my mother, and the quiet, familiar surroundings of home! I did not need a leg that had been broken some three weeks previously to be "reset". Especially when the resetting was an irreversible, crippling procedure!

I remember waking up, probably the morning after the day I arrived at this hospital. I was in a cot with high sides, amongst a sea of cots. I did not know where I was. I had needs, but I couldn't define the needs. There was no-one to turn to in my distress. Confusion and insecurity attacked me. There was nobody else in the large ward – no-one to help me, no-one to tell me where I was, or what was happening.

Eventually a white-gowned team of strangers appeared: "just a little prick" and a needle was jabbed into me. So many needles had been jabbed into me already! Then, just the blackness of drugged sleep.........

My right leg, which had taken the full force of the front bumper of the speeding car, and had been gently placed in a plaster cast by Dr. Vincent, was reset under anaesthetic in the theatre of the Children's hospital.

Time was an enigma. Could it ever have been so important to an eight year old to know the time? The confusion and isolation coupled with having absolutely no idea of what the time was, how long I had been there, and how long the nightmare would continue, plagued my conscious thoughts – not to mention the lack of communication and compassion that I suffered in that dreadful place! I found myself in another ward – a busy place, with beds that were occupied to left and to right, and some children who were patients, running around the ward. Most of the time, no-one took the slightest notice of me.

However, I recalled the frightening experience I had when a team of white-clad nurses came to make my bed: the bed had to be made – *never mind the patient*! The patient was just an object in the way. A person called a "staff nurse" flaunted her authority in front of the team of juniors accompanying her by whipping me unceremoniously up off the bed, and dumping me on a nearby cupboard against a wall in the ward. The piece of furniture was terrifyingly high above the floor – higher than a regular table. It had a smooth, hard, cold, metallic surface and was no more than about twelve to fifteen inches wide – hardly room to spread my arms to balance my body. My fear of falling was overwhelming. My little arms were trembling, trying to support my half reclining upper body, while my lower body had to be supported by a newly broken leg in a tight, neat, white plaster. My left leg, bent double at the knee, with a foot like a raw steak, hung limp. It couldn't support anything. But the bed had to be made! There were rude and crude comments about the bed being wet, but not a care for the little patient who could not control her bladder. I was incontinent in the early weeks after the accident – possibly because of the hip injuries, possibly because of the aftermath of trauma, possibly because there was no way of communicating with anyone when I needed a bed pan, possibly because I was too scared to be lifted onto a pan.

The greatest agony was needing my mother, but she was nowhere in those long, long, confused and painful days. Whether before, or afterwards, I do not know, but I caught wind of the fact that "they" would not let her visit me, because I cried too much! Long live the horror of the Johannesburg Children's hospital!

Eventually my mother broke through the barriers of hospital legality, and, I still see her standing at the door of the ward. She was dressed in the fashion of the day – wearing a neat, brightly coloured floral dress over corseted waist and hips. Her figure was well proportioned, and her posture proud and upright. Her brown hair had been set in shining curls, her face was powdered, her lashes enhanced with black mascara, and her lips ruby-red with the bright coloured lipstick she always chose. She was more beautiful than her sister, and I knew that her sister had been sought after as a film star. Oh, how I needed her! I needed her beyond what tears or cries or words could explain!

I cried, "Mommy........." Could I stop the tears? Tears of the agony of wanting with my entire soul and mind; wanting, wanting, wanting so that my being was pervaded by the all-consuming want.

She held my hand with one hand, and with the other gently pushed the hair from my forehead on the left side, careful not to touch the wound on the right. "Charmazelle........."

I knew but did not understand the bond of motherhood and the agony of separation in times of trouble. I said, "I am so scared." I needed her to hold my hand, and not ever to let go!

"Why are you scared, my love?"

"They, they came – and........ took me out of my bed" I sobbed, at the horror of the memory.

I had but one survival mechanism, and that was contact with my mother. I needed the succour and protection that only she could offer. All I wanted was to hold onto her, and know that she was holding on to me. "The plaster hurts." I said indicating my right leg.

Looking at the cast, she observed, "But it is a nice, new, neat, clean plaster!" (The one they had removed was huge and ungainly and brown from the blood that had seeped through)

She sensed my deeper agony, the agony of fear, and she knew that she had to get me out of there! She perceived that she should take steps to do so. "I will not leave you again."

She quashed the protocol of the place declaring she was removing her child, pitting herself against formalities and threats, and educated opinions regarding medical care that I should have, but she got me out of that place by hook or by crook.

I was taken back home again. A full-time maid, a little black girl of about sixteen years old, called Florence, was employed to stay by my bedside, and play with me, and hand me things I might need. On sunny days my mother or father would carry me out into the garden, and place me on a "garden swing" – a piece of outside furniture, a soft-cushioned swinging couch suspended by chains from a frame. I called my little black friend Flory-mory-bom-bom. *She was the best childhood friend I ever had!*

I used to get cross with her when the pain and disability got the better of me, and I would scream at her, and tell her to call my mother. Our house was on a small farm on the outskirts of Johannesburg. My mother was a horticulturalist, and was deeply involved in the family farming venture, so she left Flory to attend to me for longer and longer periods of time. As my condition improved, I taught Flory to play chess. Oh dear! I would beat her, and beat her, and beat her. But Flory had to play chess! In those days, a wheel chair arrived, and that was great, being able to get from place to place. However, there were lots of steps, and Flory had to get me up and down the steps without tipping the wheelchair over.

The time came for the plaster to be removed from my right leg which had been broken and set in the Children's Hospital. I still remember the horror on my mother's face when she saw that leg! Not only had the leg been set with the tibia rotated so my foot was bowed inward, but the neat, tight, white plaster was put on so tight that it had gouged a huge wound into the upper side of my ankle. The tendon that flexed and extended my big toe had been damaged, so a hammer-toe resulted, and the damaging of the flexor tendon served to increase the inward curvature of my foot. This limb was the one that grew normally! But because of the damage done, when I eventually could wear shoes, it needed an even bigger shoe to accommodate the misshapen foot. My left leg which had stopped growing having been paralysed by the first lot of hospital staff, made the inequality even greater!

Medical negligence *par excellence*!

The whole episode had to be relived again and again to gather information for the court case, and I had to undergo medical examination after medical examination which was not pleasant. I remember in particular that one of the doctors I was under used a pin to prick my left leg, and monitor the growth of the nerves. I learned that there were motor nerves which control movement and sensory nerves which identify sensation. Nerves grow very slowly – one millimetre per given period of time which I forget. Slowly over the months, sensation crept down the leg, and eventually, very weakly into the foot and then the toes; but the motor nerves never really recovered – the ankle remained cemented turning the foot inwards, and the toes remained clawed from the ankylosis.

The motorist's Third Party Insurers were the defendants for the case, and they also had their medical team who had to be satisfied. Much of the claim was finally refuted on the grounds that the permanent disability was not caused by the motor accident, but by subsequent action on behalf of the medical people who were involved with the aftercare. My parents were told rather to sue the Provincial Administration. The case, which was scheduled to be heard in the Supreme Court of Johannesburg, was settled out of court, minutes before the hearing was to start, for a fraction of the amount for which summons had been issued.

The accident had happened on the fifth of May that year, 1950. I had really only had one term in standard two (now known as grade four). I never went back to school that year. However, they promoted me to standard three.

In standard four, our little, old, but very strict maths teacher, made the announcement to the class:

"You know girls, Charmazelle is the best girl in this class at arithmetic!"

Did it help me? Children are cruel. They don't want to play with disabled children, who hobble in boots and irons! They certainly don't show any kindness or sympathy. The cripple who tags along behind, has to do so on his or her own steam. No-one gives a glance backward to show they care, and certainly no-one stretches out a hand and says,

"Come, take my hand. I will help you over the rough parts."

I was rejected, an outcast. I remember the emotional hurt of this much, much more than the physical pain or inconvenience of the deformities.

My grandmother, whose resources were often better than that of my parents, paid for one pair of "orthopaedic boots" after another. The orthopaedic boot makers in my life had as much a lesson to learn in their departments as the medics of this saga. I would agonise trying to walk in one horrible, ugly, ungainly pair of boots after another.

But......... *I found other wings to fly*!

THREE

THE HORSE

Prior to the accident, when I was about six years old, a flashy gentleman had arrived at our country home one day, riding a horse. He was a picture of the cowboy of the Western movies – tall and slim, but well-muscled, with confident stride and stature. Knee-high boots, leather chaps over jeans, a checked shirt and large Stetson-type hat completed the portrayal of a star of the great West. He had come to sell his horse to my mother. A military saddle and outrageous bridle were included in the price. The saddle was enormously heavy, and most unfashionable. It was made out of coarse, dark leather, moulded over a huge iron pommel, fitted with ungainly leathern loops for stirrups. The bridle had heavy brass buckles and decorative, serrated, round brass fittings which attached the brow-band to the headpiece. The Pelham bit had long shanks and a heavy curb chain that the Cowboy fastened unnecessarily tightly to control the horse. The entire bitting arrangement no doubt hurt the horse, and this hardened his mouth to a point, where in some circumstances he would be quite uncontrollable. Mojiek was a bright chestnut in colour, with a wide, white blaze, running from nostril to forelock on his face. He had huge, brown, frightened eyes. He stood about fifteen two hands high, and was very thick-set. Having been gelded late, his neck and forequarter were over developed, and his girth was probably far bigger than that of a horse that stood much higher.

My mother would mount the horse, and my father would lift me into the saddle up front of her for us to ride to the school bus stop in the early mornings. I remember one morning, as we cantered from our property, Mojiek showed his form by bucking us both off!

Some time after the accident, probably a year or two, when my body regained a measure of the strength after the shock, and the drugs, my father lifted me, once again, onto Mojiek. Flory was taught to hold the rein, and lead the horse at a walk. It takes time to regain the balance and confidence and strength needed to ride a horse. By the same token, riding the horse infused balance, confidence and strength to an injured body. The exercise imparted new life to me. Astride the horse I had new hope. A new vista, a new prospect, a new outlook was defined in my mind, and, greatest of all a new challenge presented itself.

My mother no doubt realised that Mojiek was far too big and strong for me to ride off the lead, and so she searched for a pony that I could handle. She found a pony owned by a family of Russian origin who lived not far from us. This little number stood about fourteen one hands high and was a flea bitten light bay (the jargon for a spray of white flecks, mainly on the rump and shoulder of a light brown horse). The Russian introduced himself as Vladimir, and we also met his beautiful daughter, Nadya. The Russian was of formidable stature and looked like a giant to me. He had olive skin, a flashy, dark moustache, and dark green-black eyes. Nadya, a tall, willowy girl in her late teens, was an accomplished rider. She had ridden Sandra successfully in children's show jumping classes, and highly commended the pony.

"She never says no to a jump! I used to ride with my friend, Yvonne. We cantered through the suburbs, jumping one garden wall and fence after another."

I gave an exclamation of amazement. Nadya was so much to be admired! She had the same olive skin as her father, and it was most becoming. Her arms and legs were slender, and her movements graceful. Her lovely face was delicately framed by a fleece of nutty-brown curls. This lovely girl was everything I wanted to be – a poised teenager with confident smile and the positive attitude of being absolutely what she wanted to be. I looked up at her as a crippled eight year old, who had seen trauma most would never see – and she smiled down at me. Nadya became my role model!

My mother shared briefly the story of the accident with Vladimir and his wife; in part, an explanation of why she wanted to buy a pony for me. They discussed rehabilitation and the therapeutic value of horse riding.

"My oldest son," Vladmir said, "Had *osteomyletis*.......... They were going to amputate his leg at the hip."

"And?" mother was horrified.

"He's fine now. Healed."

"That's wonderful! How was he healed?"

"Aah........." Vladmir uttered, as if reluctant to mention a well kept secret. "Your daughter can be healed as well!"

It was some time after this conversation that a spiritualist, named Erbshite, was ushered up to my bedroom one evening. My mother introduced him, and he sat on a chair by my bedside.

By way of explanation she said: "Her legs were badly injured – and, she wakes up screaming many times through the night."

My left leg was strapped into some orthopaedic contraption to try and keep the knee straight while I slept, and the toes were strapped onto a foot piece, in the hope of correcting the clawing. The right leg was in plaster – more inaccessible. The man mumbled something, and in a trancelike attitude, fluttered his hands up and down the length of my left leg, and then proceeded with the ritual, fluttering over the plaster on the other leg.

My mother was quite delighted the next day. She said that that night was the first night I had slept through since the accident.

*   *   *

Eventually I rode Sandra on my own, but I never really came to grips with that pony. She was clever and cunning, and normally devised a plan to run away with me, or toss me off her back. Her previous mistress was strong and much older than I. The pony was used to this mastery; and she was clever enough to know that I was no match for her. During one of my subsequent spells in hospital, this naughty little mare was disposed of by my parents.

Mojiek was still there, and I turned to him. He was sincerely honest, and not in the least bit wily. Although he was very strong I could bargain for a measure of safety when riding him. This horse had never been schooled, and I knew precious little about balancing a horse on different legs at the canter. Mojiek would simply shoot off on the off fore, and there was little that could be done to change the habit. In the years during which I had to learn to walk again, between the series of operations to try and straighten my crooked legs and feet, Mojiek was a therapist bar none. His frightened eye was tempered with time to reflect an expression of trust and faithfulness.

It was a time for rejoicing in a manner of speaking – for I could move, move to cover the earth with other legs, move from place to place without the debacle of deformed feet. There was freedom when my hair was swept from my face in the wind. There was freedom from the imprisonment of being a cripple. There was an activity in which I could excel, I could better my peers; I could fly from the agony of being an outcast!

"Oh, if they could see me now!" I thought as I galloped the grasslands of the Highveld. "I can go where they cannot go. I can be what they are not.

I don't have to hear and bear the monotone *'we can't play with you, because you might hurt your legs.'*"

I was about thirteen when Cheeko arrived. Cheeko was perfect. He was a fourteen one hand dun gelding. We had him bitted in a vulcanite Pelham with joiners, and I could hold him easily with a single rein. By this time the huge, impractical military saddle had been replaced with something more practical. I rode Cheeko backwards and forwards across the undeveloped grasslands beyond the northern suburbs of greater Johannesburg. I hunted on him with the Rand Hunt Club. I rode gymkhanas. I rode to the riding school some miles away to have "lessons" that my parents never paid for, because they did not think I needed lessons. I rode through the suburbs to shows. I jumped in all the classes I could enter for. I had wings that no other had, and I could move without pain, and hold my own in a competitive world.

However, the euphoria of *the horse* was not a constant state of mind. There were shadows that lengthened, and darkened, waned and disappeared; only to appear again more intensely. The shadows were the substance of loneliness and fear and instability, beckoning to a darkness I could not identify.........

If Cheeko was perfect in earthly terms, Moonlight Gambler, the horse I got when I was fifteen, was fashioned in the heavenlies. He was a steed to surf the skies......... The only white marking this fifteen two hand, dark bay Anglo-Arab had was a tiny star on the forehead. I was overawed with everything about him. He covered the ground with poetic cadence, rhythm, symmetry. Softness and suppleness, featured in his every stride; suppleness in his body, and willingness in his mind. He had a snaffle mouth, and by the time I was in my mid teens, I had learnt enough about horses to know that that was the only bit for a youngster. I literally roamed the earth on Gambler, covering ground as never before; enjoying the buoyancy of his trot, as he floated, seemingly above the ground; revelling in the lightness of his canter as he covered ground with eager strides.

In my matric year, at the age of fifteen, I fell in love. This was seven years after meeting Nadya, the lissom teenager I had so admired and had hero worshipped as a child. She was a girl of exceptional beauty, and absolutely feminine; but Duncan, the boy I loved, who had similar coloring, nutty brown hair, green eyes, and an olive skin, had the naughtiness, physique and chivalrous attitude that was absolutely macho. He flaunted a shock of wavy hair that fell over his forehead, and accentuated a special sparkle in his eye. At seventeen he was well muscled, but tall and slim; and he carried himself with good posture and a profound step. When we first met a fire was ignited that burned with the fervour of young love. We relished each other's company at college; studying, rushing to eat a toasted cheese sandwich and drink a cup of hot coffee at break time, holding hands in the passages between classes, and enjoying the dimension of the powerful attraction we had one for another. He was repeating matric, where-as I had jumped from standard eight, having skipped standard nine, and skipped not only a grade, but skipped right out of the girls school, where I had been unhappy for years. My beloved Duncan was very intelligent, but was unable to cope with writing exams, hence his second try.

In the summer holidays, Gambler would whisk me cross country to the house of my loved-one. The horse was so special to me in those halcyon days. I would ride him over miles of veld, across a main road, down to a river, where we snaked from property to property, jumping fences until we reached a crossing that brought us through to different territory; and then uphill via footpaths in the veld to another main, tarred road. There, I would settle the horse to float in his extended trot, along the grassy paths at the side of the road, until we reached the turn off to the country estate where the boy of my dreams lived.

We would drink in stolen moments of young love and passion. These surreptitious visits were made over a period of many years, as he did not want his parents to know that a girl was visiting him, when all the while he should have been studying.

*　　*　　*

On my bookshelf there was a book entitled, "Training the Young Horse to Jump", and several other publications with similar context. Oh, I had read the theory, but when I cantered Gambler out over the wet grass after early spring rains, and his hoof touched the earth so lightly that we could have been flying, I did not need to go through the protocol when we reached hunt country. Gambler knew how to jump before I taught him! Huge tracts of real estate within riding distance of our property were strewn with jumps erected by the Rand Hunt Club. Barbed wire fences were built into fixed wooden hencoops, and one could jump from one undeveloped property to another, on country tracks and paths, through veld and vlei, without the restriction of boundaries. All these places were my homeland. I trotted, cantered and galloped through terrain that was mine, despite there being no title deed. I loved Duncan, but I shared my passion for him with another passion, and that was jumping!

Nadya's friend, Yvonne lived a few miles from us in a beautiful country home, on a well manicured estate. She had said that I could practice in her jumping paddock, which was equipped with a proper set of show jumps. On a lonely afternoon, I arrived there, and thrilled to the occasion of putting my beloved horse to flight over the course of jumps. A philosopher of an earlier age spoke of an inbuilt, elevated image in man that is created by the horse. When Gambler jumped I was elevated to another realm. I had already put in my entries to compete in show jumping events at the Rand Easter Show, and I was looking forward to this event with all my heart.

The sunlight playing on the grassed jumping paddock lost its shimmer of green, as clouds above obscured the sun. The clouds darkened quickly, and a wind that blows a bad omen came up. There would be a storm before evening. I needed to jump a few fences once more, before turning to the gate, and the pathway home......... Yvonne and her family were out. I was alone in the jumping paddock with no tutor, no guidance. My keenness and lack of wisdom caused me to turn Gambler in to a wall that must have stood between four foot six and five feet. Gambler was a four year old, rising five, and asking him to jump that wall was taking him up too quickly. He refused because I over faced him. I approached the wall to jump it again several times, but he refused again and again; then I tried a smaller jump that we had cleared earlier, but he would not jump. In fact in the weeks to come, he would not jump at all! Gambler's confidence had been damaged, and my heart was aching. I was passionate about jumping in the Rand Show, so I took the horse all the way there, and prayed, although I knew so little about prayer. I said to God, "If Gambler jumps again, I will believe in You".

That was in the year after my matric year, I was sixteen and a half years old, and a student at Wits University. My mind was far more focused on jumping Gambler at the adjacent Rand Show Grounds, than on scientific formulae and mathematical equations. It was hard to cope with the hurt that Gambler's eagerness to jump had been undermined, and it was all my fault!

Then, on the set day, at a given time, I entered the main arena of the show grounds. My name and my horse's name were called on the public address system, the bell rang, and then......... Gambler jumped! I was amazed, overawed, grateful beyond words. We did not finish the course, but we started it. My victory was in clearing even one or two jumps. Gambler jumped and my spirit soared within me!

*   *   *

Some years later, Duncan invited me to partner him to a ball, and I was quite immersed in preparations to have my hair done, choose a beautiful dress, and do all the things a young girl does when looking forward to a great date. In those years Gina Lollobrigida was a revered film star. I thought her face was utterly beautiful, but what impressed me most about her was her high, arched eyebrows. I followed suit. My right eyebrow had been stitched at a wild angle running toward my forehead after my accident, and I trained my left eyebrow upward, to the follow the form of the other. My grandmother said I could choose a ball gown and book it to her account at one of the up-market Johannesburg fashion shops. Long gowns were out of fashion in those years. The glossy magazines featured knee length evening wear, and that is what the girls were wearing! I chose a cream brocade dress cut beautifully to a V neckline that enhanced my bust. The princess style fitted tightly at the waist, and the skirt flared out, cut to knee length. I was at the age when I knew Marilyn Monroe's vital statistics; and I knew that mine were the same. A problem arose when I took the dress home, tried it on a second time, and walked in front of a full length mirror. Although by this time I could wear shoes bought in a shoe shop, I couldn't really manage with even a little high heel. (And stiletto heels were in!) I could manage to walk in shoes with a tiny wedge heel, (and I had to think about the lessons in gratitude that I had had, given the fact that there were paraplegics who could not walk at all) but the problem with walking was that with each step my body swayed from side to side. I had been complaining of backache for some time. The doctors found that I had scoliosis of the spine as a result of the inequality of my leg lengths. I could put up with the pain of the back ache, but I was not prepared to accept the rocking of my body from side to side, which was a feature of one step on a short leg, and one step on a longer leg. That, to me, was most unattractive! It horrified me, particularly at an age where self consciousness is such an issue.

The ball was over, and some days went by. Again, I complained to my mother about backache.

She suggested: "We must get an orthopaedic boot maker to build up the left shoe."

The suggestion was positively unacceptable to me, "It won't work!" I moaned. My opinion of orthopaedic boot makers was that everything they produced was very ugly and exceedingly uncomfortable.

I continued to brood over the problem. There must be another way.........

Then, at the age of eighteen I made a bad decision. "I want to make an appointment with Dr. Fletcher." I told my mother. "I want to know what is involved in shortening my right leg."

In the days before the operation, I would burst into tears at strange times, without any provocation. Just the thought of what lay ahead caused emotional pain that I found difficult to cope with. But I was resolute, in a way, so to speak, that there is no turning back once you have put your shoulder to the plough.

Analgesics and post-operative care were either non-existent or inadequate in the year 1960 and I suffered pain of horrible proportion in the days after the operation. The operation was infinitely worse than I ever imagined it would be. Through the days of intense suffering I held on to my love for Duncan. Sometimes I felt that my love for him, and his love for me was all that kept me going. He made a few brief visits to me, during the limited official visiting times stipulated by the hospital regulations, and his presence was precious balm to me during the traumatic time.

"I have had this done for you." I said. I didn't want him to have a girlfriend who was crippled. I wanted to be beautiful and perfect for him.

"No, not for me, for yourself." He held my hand, but I believe found it difficult to come to terms with my ordeal.

The shock I received after the operation was that they had put a steel plate into my leg which was screwed into the two parts of the tibia to hold the bone in place. I had not even known that steel could be used in surgery, and, *I rejected the foreign body in my mind.*

Dr Fletcher had said that I would have pain for three days after the operation, and after three months, the plaster could be removed. I had made a calculated evaluation of his words, and worked out that I could bear it. However, the course of events was not as he had stated. The wound did not heal, and after six months, the plate was removed surgically. This operation, I recall, was even more painful than the first. Altogether I was in plaster for nine months, and the scenario was nine months of pain. My calculations were refuted.

During this time the radiant, iridescent, multifaceted, divergent rays of light, as reflected through a prism in glorious colours, that was the love between Duncan and I, faded to a nebulous monotone; and with it came pain – the pain of loss of a relationship so precious. I tried with thought and deed to hold on, and on, but I read the signs and trembled when I felt the first faint fluttering of the fact that Duncan's life was being steered on a route divergent from mine. I could not ride Gambler to visit him because my leg was in plaster, and his phone calls and visits were becoming scarcer and scarcer.

When eventually the plaster cast was removed from my leg, the incision still had not healed, and I was told that I had chronic *osteomyletis*.

FOUR

GET A WORD ABOUT BAPTISM

At the age of twenty, I was in England when I dreamt about Tim. In the dream I stood in his arms in the beautiful garden of my parent's property, just outside the front door of their stately double storey home. He was tall and broad shouldered, with blue eyes, and had a shock of light brown, curly hair. As we stood together, and without anything said, I knew that I knew this was the man I would marry. I felt secure in the calm assurance that he was not going to be snatched from me by circumstances at any moment. There was the peace of knowing that there would be permanence in our relationship; and it was good to have the courage to love, knowing that loving was not in vain.

Tim and I bought an undeveloped 20 acres of land on the South Coast of Natal – the chief attribute of this property being that it had stunning sea and inland views, and three springs with running water. We built a cottage with our own hands, shaped a garden around it, and planted windbreaks and nut trees in parts of the remaining steep lands. A row of gum trees was planted on the south-west side to protect the dwelling from the prevailing wind that rose to gale force at times of the year; and a rough garden was fashioned around the cottage, with lawns, flower beds, shrubs and trees. The original farm was called *Sanderstead,* and although we only owned a portion of the greater farm, we always referred to our property that by that name.

Three children were born of my marriage with Timothy Bryant.

Our two girls, Lucinda and Jill were about five and four years old respectively, and our son had not yet been thought about, when Tim came home one night, shouting excitedly: "Your leg can be healed!" Tim never could pronounce the word *osteomyletis*.

I raised my eyebrows higher than they were already arched, and uttered a querulous, "Oh?"

"Yes," He said, "A customer came into my shop asking for help to have a film put in his camera. I was busy with a deadline job to produce a cinema slide for a commercial company, so I told my young assistant to put the film in the camera, but she couldn't. I was working at the desk behind the screen at the back of the counter, and said that I was cursing myself for promising a job with a four o'clock deadline, which was impossible to finish by that time! A calm, soft voice came from the customer's side of the counter, *"Don't curse. Pray."*

"And then?" I was interested to hear more.

"He said there was an evangelist in town, who had grown up in the rough southern suburbs of Johannesburg. He was a toughie, who had been brought out of drug addiction, and his life had been changed. There is a week-long campaign at a local church, and we have been invited to go and listen to him. Apparently there have been miracles, some-one got up from a wheelchair, and others have been healed. I want to take you there! *Your leg can be healed!*"

Tim took me to the small country church where the evangelist was preaching during the remaining nights of that week. Without a doubt I

wanted the healing of the disease that had caused the wound in my right
leg to suppurate since I was eighteen years old. On the night of my first visit
to the Full Gospel Church, I went up into the prayer line after the message,
and the evangelist laid hands on my head and prayed. A warm current went
through my body – calming and rejuvenating. I expected the wound in
my leg to heal instantaneously, but that did not happen. Later, during that
meeting he asked who was ready to make a commitment of their lives to
Christ. My hand shot up involuntarily.

Clearly and decisively, albeit silently, I said to myself: *"Surrender, surrender,
surrender."*

The following night, I again found myself in the queue for healing. But
when my turn came to be prayed for, I was too timid to ask for what I really
wanted, lest I did not get it, so I asked for faith to be healed.

That night I supernaturally received the gift of faith, and this was to stand
me in good stead for many healings for myself and my family in the future.

Within a few weeks, Tim said: "We have to get baptized."

I did not haggle, reasoning why, but said, "If you say so."

We were baptized in the sea, one Sunday after a church service. We came
out of the water singly. I saw Tim, some distance off, kneeling in the shallow
water of approaching and receding waves, and there was some-one kneeling
beside him, but it was not the pastor who had baptised us. I also knelt at the
water's edge, closed my eyes, and prayed. Shortly I was aware of some-one
close by. A fair haired man, well tanned, in swimming trunks, knelt down
beside me and prayed with me. He spoke a few words, and then I remember
he laid hands on my head. He prayed that I might receive the gift of the
Holy Ghost and speak with new tongues, as he had done for Tim. I opened
my mouth and uttered the first few, faltering words of what sounded like
nonsense, and then, slowly, the heavenly tongue began to flow......... Later

Rob Knight introduced himself, and encouraged us. It was an appointment arranged in the heavenlies. In years to come, when thinking back on this occasion, I know that he had appeared at our sides because God had told him to be there at the time Tim and I came out of the waters.

In the coming weeks, we heard a ripple amongst the congregation: "A man and his wife were baptized in the sea and came out speaking in new tongues."

*   *   *

Tim and I ran two photographic businesses in two adjacent South Coast towns. I found it difficult to understand why, after several good years, during which we added equipment and improvements to the businesses, lately money had become incredibly tight. For some months I worked with a hint of desperation in my tempo, trying to outdo the tide, unaware that our businesses had had their heyday, and that we were now facing the twin economic horrors of inflation and the devaluation of the South African rand, the international value of which had remained static prior to the 1948 Bretton Woods Agreement. The rand was now "floating" albeit perilously in the international market, at the whim of the engineers of economic boom and recession.

Some months after we were baptized, I conceived my third child, our son, Sydney. With the additional cost of staff at my shop during the later months of my pregnancy, and the costs of the confinement, we found our businesses faltering for funds. However, we went ahead with our plans to add a wing to the house, with a main bedroom, bathroom, and a darkroom where the photo processing could be done at home, to avoid Tim having to stay at the shop until late hours of the night.

We had become firm friends with Rob Knight, and his lovely fair skinned, brunette wife, Dalene. They also had a family of young children, and Dalene carried her fourth child, while I carried my third.

Two or three years went by. Tim and I held tenaciously to our dreams of improving our businesses, and increasing the turnover to create more liquidity.

On one particular Sunday, after a sumptuous lunch, in the Christian custom of bringing and sharing, Rob and Dalene sat with Tim and I in our lounge and chatted. Children ran backwards and forwards with shouts of glee, enjoying games with one another. Tea had come and gone. I was half reclining on the couch. The old wound on my right shin was in full view. I swished a fly from the weeping sinus.

Others had prayed. Could there be a result if Rob prayed? I asked myself.

Rob had been silent for some time. He sat on a chair close to the couch, and could see my misshapen feet, wasted calves, scarred lower legs, and the suppurating wound.

I couldn't help saying: "I so want the wound to heal. It has been open for nearly twenty years."

Rob spoke, but not to me. He addressed the injured leg: "You spirit of osteomyletis, I bind you in the name of Jesus!"

This was one of many statements that Rob made, which I rejected for want of understanding. How much time it takes for the great truths pertaining to vital spiritual issues to dawn!

*   *   *

After some time, when we were alone together, I told Tim "At first it was only the faintest wisp of a memory, and then I relived the ordeal, and now the truth is shouted from the mountain top: *the spiritualist, Erbshite*! He did his hocus-pocus, fluttering his hands over my legs those many years ago. He brought that spirit hot from the press, from the boy he had 'healed' – *the spirit of osteomyletis.* I lived with the fear of the disease for ten years, and then I contracted it. QED. I once had a maths teacher who taught me that means *quod erat demonstrandum* after an equation is solved. We kids were taught the translation: *quite easily done.*"

"So the healing has to be in the realm of the spirit, before it is manifest in the flesh." Tim observed.

I was excited. "This explains why, although we have prayed so often, I have never got the healing! What a relief to know this. Now I have hope."

There continued to be milestones in the healing process. One night when I was putting my little girls to bed, Lucy had been restless. I sat by her bed and sang gospel songs to soothe her to sleep. Then, for some time after the child had fallen asleep, I continued to sing and praise the Lord. Then I stopped singing, and in the darkness and silence of my daughter's bedroom, I started praying about my leg wound. Soon I heard a definable inner voice:

"Go in peace. You are healed."

I rejoiced in the spirit but there was no change in the flesh. The wound continued to flare up and fester resulting in a mental conflict between that which I could see and that which was the substance of faith. On another occasion we were at a fellowship meeting on a Saturday night. A circle of believers sang and praised the Lord with gospel songs. Suddenly I felt a throbbing in the tissue of the dead flesh around the sinus. We had been singing about the blood of Jesus. In the spirit, I visualised that blood flowing, restoring, renewing, bringing new life to dead flesh.

It is easy to forget the promises of God, and accept what the eye can see. As there was still no visible sign of improvement, there were times when my hope wore thin. However, the flicker that remained was important. All was not lost. Had it not been for the continuing, frail thread of hope, there would be no testimony. During the years that followed the promise of a better condition was nurtured, however unattainable that promise might have been. There was that realm to aspire to while hope remained; there was the evidence of things unseen that could still be embraced while the frail, silvern thread remained intact.

When I was thirteen I had been taught to "accept" my condition. As a result of this I had formed a stoical attitude, and gritted my teeth silently in many a cul-de-sac. I felt, at times, it would have been easier to fall back on this resource, than to continue holding so defiantly on to my little bit of hope. A conflict raged within me. No doubt, as a result of the power of God working within me, I was not prepared to compromise my faith for my former state of mind. I held on, and on......... and the scenario was that the greater my expectation for a miracle, the greater was my disappointment at the sight of the flesh.

One Sunday afternoon, we Bryants were seated comfortably in the spacious lounge of the Knight's home. The furnishings, in mellow shades of cream and beige complemented the restful atmosphere. People were conversing happily. Children darted back and forth, intent on their purposes.

However, despite the friendliness and Christian love, I was not relaxed and happy. I was exceedingly troubled on two fronts: that the healing of my leg had not taken place despite prayers and promises which I believe I had heard, and the unexpected turn that the finances of our businesses had taken exposing a most insecure state of affairs. The feeling of unrest about these matters was apparent, but was there another latent matter that contributed to my lack of peace and joy? I thought that a cigarette would help, but I decided against lighting up, as I would have been the only one who was smoking. I participated less and less in the conversation around me, and turned my thoughts inward, there to roam dark and shady avenues, where grotesque, giant trees obscured the light. Dark areas beneath the leafy masses stole clarity from my pathway; undefined elements were impeding my path, as if to crush my endeavours and halt my progress. Was I veering from the norm of sanity, or were these signs indicative of the fact that my life was heading for a cataclysm?

I wanted to escape from the Knight's lounge – to leave, to go; to disappear regardless of being rude and breaking a good friendship. I was wondering how I could tear Tim and the children away from the afternoon visit. How could I do this without creating a scene? I battled with thoughts of getting away for some time, and then, involuntarily it seemed, I burst out.

"There must be something wrong between me and God!"

Having uttered the words, I chewed on the kernel: I didn't really believe there was something wrong between me and God, so why did I say it? And if there was something wrong, why couldn't I deal with the matter myself, secretly? I felt foolish and embarrassed at my words.

Rob took up the cue to reply to me, and his suggestion was premeditated for some moments, before he spoke.

"Get a word from the Lord about baptism."

"Baptism?" I was astounded. This was by no means what I expected to hear.

"Yes, burial." Rob replied.

"But we've been baptized!" I cried, remembering that day on the beach three and a half years previously.

Rob did not answer. No doubt he would rather wait for the Holy Spirit to minister understanding to me.

This is the conversation that took place on the Sunday preceding the Monday, when I asked the Lord for a word while I was working in the darkroom. And what did I hear?

"Shake off the dust from your feet."

FIVE

YOUR WOUND IS INCURABLE

I slid from the high stool in the darkroom to reach for the switch of the safe light, which would swathe the darkroom in a mellow, red glow. Then I made a mental assessment of the prints that still had to be made. I could finish by midday if I worked steadily. Continuing, I was undisturbed by the two little boys playing in the garden outside. Sydney, who was three years old three, had an "umfaan" for a friend – a little Zulu boy two or three years older than him – whom he loved playing with. The two of them would spend hours making endless tracks in the sand for toy cars and tractors. By now my maid would have given them each a biscuit and a cold drink.

While confusion disturbed me on one front of my walk as new Christian, steadfast belief in, and gratitude to God prevailed on another. Since Sydney was six months old, I understood that I was to pray for his safety every time I drove out of our front gate, and left him in the care of my young, black maid, Tamara. This prayer was always answered. During those times he was never hurt, where-as when Tim or I were with him, all the babyhood tumbles, falls, injuries and tears occurred.

It was just after midday when I left the darkroom – about an hour to go before I would collect Lucy and Jill from school. I walked out into the garden. The air was fresh and moist, expectant with the first warmth of spring. I walked a little further from the house to sit for a while on a rickety bench in the shade of a tree. Tim had planted that tree. I looked about to embrace the spectre of what my husband and I had achieved in the last ten years. The nut trees that we had planted in the valleys had died, as the three springs had dried up, and, although I had not counted the years, it seemed we had been through a seven year drought. We just managed to keep the garden around the house intact. The veld beyond its border was a taskmaster on its own, devouring most things we planted further out. The house was liveable although it never reached the status of the house of our dreams, but we had had to work within perimeters that we could afford. What it lacked in professional finish was made up for in rustic charm. We had laid many of the concrete blocks personally, and I was the artist and the artisan behind the Spanish plaster that covered the outside walls. A Spanish plastered house was very much more elegant than a house with a façade of concrete block. There is a bond between an artist and his work – a stirring element of satisfaction, a pride that leaves a warm glow in the heart.........

I thought back at the time when Sydney was two months old, and I was up on the scaffold, constructing Spanish Style arches that would add grace and stature to the house. Concurrent with the building of the arches, an extra wing was added, comprising a master bedroom, bathroom, and darkroom.

Now that the arches had been completed and painted, and embroidered with the traditional row of red, clay, corrugated tiles atop, the place looked very much more palatial than the original concrete block cottage. Standing tall against a background of blue-green gum trees, and azure sky, I had to admit the place looked good as it neared completion after all these years. We would not have swapped our farm style dwelling on an isolated hilltop for suburban elegance, and our children were used to the challenges and freedom of the countryside. This was the only home that they had ever known.

Tim and I had put all our resources into the place, and it stood to our credit threefold: as a dwelling place, as an investment, and as an artwork created by us. It was safe. My father had always taught me that brick and mortar was the safest investment. Resting firmly in the conviction that this asset could not be shaken, I shivered slightly as I sat on that bench under the tree. Did I feel the first, faint beginnings of a tremor that spelled calamity? There was a strange undercurrent that I could not define. What was meant by *"Shake off the dust from your feet"?* Was the dust the dry soil of this land, this land we had toiled over in the days of our youth?

Our two photographic businesses functioned on imported raw materials, as neither film nor photo chemicals were manufactured in South Africa. The sudden rise in the cost of raw materials came as a shock. The increased price was, of course, brought about by the devaluation of the rand on the international market. Tim and I did not understand what had happened. Not only did our production costs loom to a new high, but there was another prevalent economic rot responsible for reduced sales. The South Coast town of Port Shepstone in which we lived survived on the activities of the sugar cane farmers, and the Umzimkulu Mill which was the tick-tock that throbbed economic life into the area. The drought had hit the farmers!

So our chief product, the luxury item, portraiture, became less and less sought after; the sales of art works, picture frames and other products that we stocked also declined radically. We had chiselled our staff down from twelve to two, and had literally given away the business operating from the Margate outlet. We consolidated to one outlet, and did the photo processing at home to enable us to reduce costs and be there for our children.

In order to supply the working capital and improved equipment that was needed, we took out a mortgage bond on our property. Tim and I firmly, if naively believed that if we continued to take excellent photographs, and coupled this with new ideas, technical advancements and continued hard work, we would break through the bad patch. We shared a tangible vision of success.

*   *   *

My parents had disposed of their Johannesburg properties to buy a sugar cane farm, situated about ten kilometres from *Sanderstead*. I had always had a particular rapport with my kid sister, Pauline, who was not much older than my first born, Lucy. Pauline's passion was show jumping, and as a child, she had won boxes of rosettes, mainly red, which was the colour allotted for first place by the show holding bodies on the South Coast. It was always Pauline's intention to give her show pony, Rommel to Lucy when she outgrew him. In time Pauline acquired a bigger horse to compete in junior classes. This horse was a bright chestnut with a narrow blaze and three white socks. My mother named him Duhallow. There was thoroughbred prominent in his breeding, but he had the feathered fetlocks of a cross-breed. He was as hot a number, as a chestnut with white points can be; he could as nearly soar like an eagle as it was possible for a horse to do. He would jump anything he was ever faced at. Pauline and I both knew that he had it in him to make *JA*, which was the top junior grade in show jumping. In the show ring Duhallow seldom knocked a jump, and could turn on a tickey. He was lunged regularly to keep the level of fitness needed for competition; and he was very well schooled which enabled him to maintain the balance needed in the sport. Duhallow's biggest fault was his zeal. He would plunge and leap forward on approaching a fence, which made it difficult to place his take-off. However he had a sufficiently powerful jump in him to clear a four foot six oxer, even if he took off a stride to soon; and he was athletic enough to clear a fence of that size if he approached too close – *got under it*, in the jargon. Tending to be over-impulsive, as he was, it required courage, skill and strength to channel his energy in an arena. On an outride, he was also hot. At the canter he would playfully do flying changes on the straight, striving all the while to lengthen to a gallop – and then there was fire in his stride.

I had never ridden Duhallow. I was a little in awe of the horse; also having had three babies in the past few years, I was out of practice and I needed to tone my muscles and rejuvenate my confidence. I knew that the horse would be too much of a handful for me, so I did not even entertain thoughts of riding him. He was a horse for some-one far younger and fitter and a better rider than I. Pauline was in line for receiving inter-provincial colours in show jumping – I had not ever come near to such a prestigious accomplishment.

However, Pauline's show jumping era ended abruptly, just before she should have reached the summit in her sport. One day when I was visiting my family, she rushed into the lounge.

"Duhallow is sick!" She cried.

"Let's go down to the stables." My voice echoed concern.

We walked together.

When I saw the horse, I said: "He's got that sick look about him."

"His eyes are big and watery, and his ears flop to either side." Pauline remarked.

We went into the stable to look at him more closely. He was a horse that was responsive to love and to the voice of his owner.

"His spine seems so prominent, and his coat doesn't have the lustre it should have. I think we had better call a vet!" I said.

Before the vet came to examine Duhallow, I had to go home, but Pauline phoned me to tell me what his diagnosis was.

"Duhallow is very ill. He has a disease of the liver, called senecciosis. It is caused by eating excess amounts of a plant that has small, yellow, daisy-like flowers. I haven't seen any on our farm, but he could have eaten the plant years ago, and only got sick now."

"And what can they do?" I asked.

"Nothing." The vet said he would be dead in twelve to eighteen months.

"A terminal disease! I am shocked!"

"Sounds like it."

I could hear Pauline sobbing on the phone. "I am so very, very sorry." What more could I say?

"He has given me a course of pep-up injections that will stimulate the liver, and there will be a temporary improvement in his condition. It is a course of five doses that has to be injected into the soft flesh of his chest. Will you come and do the injections for me?"

"Yes, of course!" I assured her.

*   *   *

Tyrone and Gaye Summers, the son and daughter-in-law of the elderly pastor at the Shelley Beach church at which we fellowshipped, requested that we photograph their daughter, Angela for a magazine competition. The child was a petite, pretty five year old; and the competition was to feature a little girl with a peaches-and-cream complexion. Gaye felt that this could best be portrayed if Angela was photographed with a puppy or a pony. Tim agreed that this would provide a good contrast in textures, and we also knew that fondling an animal brings out special qualities in a child. To this end Tim invited the Summers to our home one Saturday afternoon.

Lucy and Jill saddled and bridled their ponies, and made them perform all sorts of acts of obedience to set the scene for a prize-winning photograph of little Angela. After exhausting combinations of sun and flash, standard and telephoto lenses, smiles and frowns, the children were left to play in the garden and the grown-ups went inside to drink tea. Between pouring hot rounds of tea, I settled down to smoke several cigarettes, which I needed after the photo session.

The conversation homed in on the Word of God, as it so often does when members of the body gather together. The time of fellowship was, no doubt, God's appointment, for the Holy Spirit moved among us, and we discerned His precious presence. After sharing testimonies, we had a short time of prayer followed by a time of silence; each person knew that they themselves, and the others with them, were waiting on the Lord. After a while Gaye got up and walked straight over to me. She laid hands on my head.

"I feel led to pray for you." She said

I nodded.

Then Gaye started speaking in a strange tongue; praying in the Spirit of things we did not know, nor could understand, but that would be conveyed to my spirit.

I trembled. In my heart I was praising God.

Gaye's prayer continued in English: "... that you will be a vessel, full and overflowing, fit to work for the kingdom of God; that you will be clean by the word He has spoken – and that He will lead you to some-one who will be able to minister deliverance to you, that you may be set free."

Tyrone and Gaye lived in Durban – more than a hundred kilometres from us. It was to be almost seven months before we would see them again, and little did I know (nor could have coped with) the knowledge of what would happen in my life between this and the next meeting with the Summers.

There was going to be a process of refining, as of the refining of gold. Only the pure metal would withstand the process, maintain its identity, increase its value, and emerge from the process burnished, precious, polished and rare. The natural me had to die – had to be buried; I had to go through the waters of baptism in Jesus' Name, and to go through the fire of the baptism of deliverance.

If it was that I took two steps forward, only to slide one step back along the way, it was because I was still holding on to the dross of my natural upbringing, fraught with a woman's emotion. But climb, I did, for I was aware that God was performing radical, miraculous changes in me. My thought processes were changing, and with each change, I knew that my thought patterns would never revert to what they were.

Although the Word of God had been marvellously opened up to me when I was born again, and although I loved and cherished the Word, the revelation that I was seeking deep down inside of me, still eluded me. There remained unanswered questions which I pondered over when wandering through dark avenues of thought. I tried to find answers to these questions in the scriptures, and, quite by chance as it seemed, I found writings on a subject that I did not know God had documented. I had to focus and refocus my eyes when I saw the words in Jeremiah chapter thirty: *incurable wound*. I would never have thought that there was anything in the bible about an incurable wound, and I read the words again and again that they might seep into my consciousness:

> "This is what the Lord says:
>   'Your *wound is incurable*,
>   Your injury beyond healing
>
> There is no-one
>   to plead your cause,
>   no remedy for your sore,
>   no healing for you…"

Jeremiah 30:12-13 NIV

SIX

A HORSE AND HIS RIDER IS AGAINST YOU

The Word of God is incredible! I was learning that when a negative state of affairs is described, it is counteracted by a positive promise. The negative value of a mindset steeped in hopelessness regarding a certain matter would give a low pressure reading far to the left on an emotional barometer, but the needle would swing to a positive high on the right by the good news that followed.

And here is the promise that follows the statement, *your wound is incurable:*

> "'But I will restore you to health
> And *heal your wounds*,'
> Declares the Lord…"

Jeremiah 30:17 NIV

I learnt that one has to take the words as if they had substance, and hold to them very tightly, as a mother would cling to a little child in a busy place. Do not let the words go; do not falter regarding the meaning; do not lose the impact of the dynamo.

However, the battle with doubt prevailed.

For some months I pondered over the prayer that Gaye had prayed. The tug of war was: should I find some-one with a deliverance ministry, or not. I had not heard of anyone in our area who exercised the gifts of the Spirit to bring healing in the realm of deliverance. I did hear of some-one near Durban who may be able to help, but I doubted whether I would go to the expense and trouble of going there, or whether I would have the courage to approach a stranger and state brazenly 'I need deliverance. Can you help?' Never! It sounds so foolish.

Time went by and one day I was talking on the phone to a fellow photographer. He told me that there was an evangelist who stayed in the area who had been used of God in deliverance. Apparently he was often out of town, but was at home at that time. I turned the matter over and over in my mind. I reckoned that I had better take the opportunity of contacting him while he was at home. Doubt was making a mockery of my thinking. Eventually I couldn't take the indecision any longer and phoned him.

"Hello......... Is that Brandon Smith?"

"It is." From his intonation one could feel one was encroaching on his time and privacy.

What on earth was I to say next?

"Yes. Can I help you?" His manner was abrupt rather than sincere.

"I would like to make an appointment to come and see you." The telephone line was no method of communication to tell him why.

"It would be better, of course, if your husband came with you."

"Yes," I started speaking, but was cut short before I could add the word 'obviously'.

"Unless there is some reason why you do not want him to be present?" His tone was becoming tolerant.

"No, not at all." I stammered, and it occurred to me that he thought I might have marital problems.

Brandon Smith set a date and time.

Tim, being the easy-going person that he was, had no qualms about accompanying me. He did not know whether or not I needed deliverance; but he was eager that I should get what was best for me, and he trusted God that the outcome would be good.

When we left to see the man, hope was ballooning in my breast, but the hope was tempered with despair. Would this be the big night? Or would there be the same disappointment I felt on the first night I went to the Shelley Beach church to ask for prayer for my leg? The anticipation was drawing my stomach muscles tight like bowstrings.

It was dark by the time we parked outside Brandon Smith's house, and Tim led the way to knock on the evangelist's door. I trembled a little. My arm was hooked through Tim's arm, and I bent my elbow as if to draw him closer. I bit my lip, and determined that I would be nonchalant.

After brief courtesies of introductions, when I again noticed how abrupt Brandon was, he led us into his office, where the three of us sat around a large desk.

Without any ceremony, Brandon looked straight at me, and said: Well! What is your problem?"

I felt like a complete fool. I was flushed with embarrassment at his forthright question. How awful! I was going to have to make this molehill in my life sound like a big mountain, in order to convince the man that I was a worthy candidate for his ministry.

"Well……… I think I need deliverance." I tried to assume a tone of self importance.

"What makes you think you need this?" Brandon was old enough to be my father, and his attitude conveyed: let's get rid of this school-girl stuff as soon as possible.

"Well………" I couldn't even think of what my problems were, much less define them. The fact that we were being crushed by an economic nutcracker; the fact that I felt a separation from God with suicidal overtones; and the fact that I had an incurable wound seemed of little importance when voiced in a few concise words. Could I say, 'I am broke and unhappy and diseased.' Hardly!

Tim helped. He explained that we were in financial trouble and that this was causing undue stress on his wife.

"I've got just the answer for you!" The evangelist boomed. He opened the top draw of his desk, and produced a book, which he brandished in the air. "This," he said, "Is a book on prosperity!"

It was not long before Tim and I gathered that he was the proud author. He recommended that Tim read the book, and mentioned that he was certain that there was spiritual meat in the subject matter that would be to our great advantage.

"I am working against time to meet a deadline to get my second book to press." He said.

That explained why he was so impatient with my case. The talk migrated from the topic of his book to that of Christian tape ministry. The latter was a subject on which he and Tim were on common ground, and that kept them talking for a little while. I had, by this time, wished that I could disappear. It was impossible to be sociable and nonchalant while the storm was raging in my breast. Did the psychological battlefield that I thought existed, really exist? Was I imagining the peril? Perhaps our impending bankruptcy was nothing but hallucination in my tired mind. Perhaps the best thing to do was just to get the hell out, go to another town, get a job somewhere! The mind had endless avenues of escape! The men went on talking about tapes. I wanted to scream and stamp my foot.

Eventually Brandon Smith turned to face me. "Now, to get back to your problem, girl, what makes you think you've got *demons?*"

I never thought he'd get back to my problem, now that he'd sold Tim a book and discussed the tape ministry. I thought the escape would be easy: he'd bid us good night, and that would be that. I had to do some quick thinking: it would be futile to tell him about Gaye's prayer that I would be led to some-one who would minister deliverance to me. It would be too long-winded for me to tell him of the dark, indefinable spirit of depression that was inexorably intertwined in my life; and if I did tell him the issue would fall on unsympathetic ears – so why bother. I had heard it said that smoking was a result of demonic entanglement, so I blurted out:

"Well, I smoke!"

The evangelist uttered a monumental sigh! Then he bellowed: "*s-m-o-k-e!*"

I could hear him thinking, 'here I am, busy finalising a book, under great pressure of time, before I leave for my next campaign, and this simple woman wastes my valuable time because she *smokes!'*

"Well, you must just give it up! I had to. I smoked for years."

"Oh" I grunted.

He formed great circles in the air with his arms to illustrate unseen offenders: "Have you got any uncontrollable, driving forces in your life? Any compulsive desires? Any sexual lust?

"No........" I was reluctant to continue the dialogue. I actually felt like telling him to go to hell, but I kept my voice even and my attitude calm, if for no other reason than to vindicate myself.

Tim stepped in to explain that there was nothing extraordinary about our situation: financial stress, depression, unhealed wounds, and more, were nothing that God could not remedy.

We rose to leave and Brandon gave me a winning smile, "Now you go home and listen to your husband!"

I did not thank him for the diagnosis, nor for the prescription for healing. Seldom had a flicker of hope been as thoroughly extinguished as was the hope I had in my heart before that visit.

*   *   *

Tim and I and our children were once again in the living room of the Knight's home. The furnishings in cream and brown were very restful, and we enjoyed the informality of the family situation. Dalene brought in a tray of refreshments, and for some time we talked about children, and the highs and lows of the past week.

Tim was telling Rob about our adventure, daring as it was at this stage of economic uncertainty, into printing our own colour photographs. Our darkroom was equipped to print black and white pictures, which was all the business catered for in the early days. Out of the meagre takings from this medium, we bravely endeavoured to finance colour printing, despite the embryonic technology that was available.

"If only the colour would come *right*!" Tim said

"Indeed?" Rob was listening attentively.

Tim continued: "I have always believed that the day we start printing out own colour, will be the day we break through into something good! We have gambled several hundred rand on a second hand enlarger, colour paper and chemicals, yet we just can't get a professional print."

I sighed for I had been told for a long time that printing our own colour was the one thing that could pull our business around. However, my faith had been worn thin by the vain promises of the salesman from the photographic supply company that had got us this far. Every time there was just another gadget that would make the difference. The spending of another two thousand rand would see the process right! I decided I had better keep quiet.

Tim continued: "I've always felt that if we could offer the public something a little better than the lab……… if I could do with colour some of the things I've done with black and white! Also we could give a quicker service."

I had to chip in, "Love, it's taking so long to get the colour photographs out now, I don't want to meet people in the street. You know what it's like in a small town. It was quicker to send the film to Durban."

"We've had technical difficulties," Tim continued, "but I still believe we can turn out a really artistic, professional job."

Rob ventured, "Would it not help to continue sending the film to the lab, until the problem is sorted out?"

"The colour bill is several hundred rand a month!" I interjected. "We were hoping to save by buying the chemicals and equipment. We need to save on something in order to keep going!"

After a while of silence Rob asked Tim, "Who handles the money in your house?"

I was so indignant at Rob's question that I walked out of the living room into the kitchen. Dalene was getting together a quick high tea, and I took refuge at the kitchen sink. Washing dishes would keep me quiet – there I could brood, unnoticed.

However, Dalene noticed me, and encouraged me to speak. "I feel so........."
How was I to explain the frustration and fear? "I feel as though I'm in the wrong place, everything's going wrong." I sounded confused and simple.

"You are seated in heavenly places with Christ Jesus." She said lovingly.

I couldn't understand why she said a thing like that, when it was obvious to me that I was where I was. I found myself unable to accept this fact by faith. I was refusing to accept the ideal because I was bound by the actual.

Although I was aware of the sincerity with which that remark was made, and I did not appreciate it at the time, in time to come I was to remember this serenely spoken truth. There were to be occasions in the future when I desperately needed to draw strength from these words.

We spent a noisy half hour feeding the children picnic style, and then gathered again in the lounge. I went to sit next to Tim. Rob was sharing something with him, and I just caught the word, '*generation*'. I picked up a bible that was lying open next to Tim. The bible was open at Exodus chapter thirty four, and I saw part of a verse standing out, as if in bold italics:

> "......visiting the iniquity of the Fathers on the children and on the children's children to the third and fourth generation..."

> Exodus 34:7

I swallowed, then said, "I think I've got something here!" and read the scripture aloud.

"Indeed?" Rob encouraged me to go on.

"I really feel that this in some way applies to me. Some members of my family have been involved in the occult."

Rob and Dalene understood, and knew that I needed to be nurtured in the love of God. After a while Dalene got up and went to the piano. She started to play, and we gathered round her in a circle and began singing songs of praise. Twilight closed in outside, and one by one the children joined the circle.

Later, in the quietness that followed the songs of praise and worship, Rob turned to Tim: "Brother, I believe that I have a word from the Lord."

"Really?" Tim was eager to hear.

"A horse and his rider is against you." Rob said, looking pertinently at me..

SEVEN

DROUGHT

One Sunday morning after a praise and worship service in the Shelley Beach church, members of the congregation were filing down the centre aisle to leave the church. Tim and I met a couple who were a few years our senior, and we spontaneously started chatting. Although it was an unusual subject to discuss with strangers in a crowded aisle, the conversation turned to business and business anxieties. Kevin and Martha had recently come to the South Coast and were exploring different possibilities to establish themselves in a new home and find a new work situation.

"We have a business for sale." Tim said

Kevin listened cautiously, and then asked "What type of business?"

"A photo business in Margate,"

"At what price?"

"You can take it over for the debts." Tim said without premeditation

"Yes!" I echoed, thinking how good it would be to shed *that* load.

There were handshakes between the four of us, as we moved forward down the aisle.

We all knew that the deal was done. A covenant had been entered into.

We passed through the door of the church, into the foyer where we shook hands with the pastor and thanked him for the service, then stepped outside into the bright sunlight and, after the appropriate goodbyes had been said, went our separate ways.

It then followed that Tim and I henceforth put our energies together in Port Shepstone. We felt that if we worked from one outlet, with a considerably reduced staff, we would be able to consolidate our operation, and increase our profit margin. This concept, although sound in logic, was never given time to bear fruit, owing to several external factors which arose unexpectedly imposing stresses that our ailing business was unable to bear.

There was only one main-line local industry, and that was the production of sugar. The sugar mill was the heart of the industry – a gigantic crushing plant that served farmers over a huge semi-circular area. It was the sole market place to which the farmers of the community brought their produce. The cane was crushed by huge rollers. The juices were purified and turned into sugar; and the sugar was railed to the Sugar Terminal at Durban harbour for export. The product was therefore also important for earning foreign exchange. From the Mill other by-products, such as molasses, were distributed to the home market. The entire local economy depended on the sure functioning of this enormous, intricate mechanism, which absorbed, processed and distributed the only crop of any consequence that was grown on the South Coast – sugar cane. The Mill was the largest employer of skilled and unskilled labour in the area – not only did it generate direct buying power to other local businesses by virtue of its wage bill, but also indirect buying power by consuming goods manufactured, sourced or procured by a spectrum of satellite businesses that served it. In their turn these many small businesses would feel the pinch of the lower world sugar price, even more than the concomitant climatic factor of the past season of drought. To add to the list of perils, in that year, 1977, there had been a major technical hitch in the completion of the Mill's maintenance program.

When the crushing season was due to start, farmers were advised not to deliver cane! This obviously had repercussions. They had held on through a long winter off-season – meeting wages and other overheads, no doubt, on bank overdraft. By the time the Mill eventually started crushing, over three million rand for cane purchases should already have been paid out. (The real value of that money as this book goes to press could more likely be three hundred million rand). The withholding of this flow of money from the community had a ripple effect that was felt by every secondary business in the string of adjacent towns and villages along the coast.

The delay in anticipated turnover hit our business at a time when we had to meet number four in a series of post dated cheques that we had issued to our bondholders. Tim and I had breathed sighs of relief as each of the first three cheques found their way through the morass of our overdrawn bank account. We held onto a faint, despairing hope that number four would dodge its way through the obstacles in the perilous flow; that it would be presented before some other cheques of lesser importance found their way through; and that if a cheque or cheques were to bounce, it would not be the mortgage one.

The locals were also feeling the effects of the drought which had not broken, and this factor was taking its toll in divers ways:

Tim summed it up: "God is withholding the rain from a stubborn and rebellious generation."

I did not disagree, but his comment gave me no consolation. At *Sanderstead* we were dependant on rain water to fill our tanks. There would be trying times ahead if the tanks ran dry. The first logical step to avert that tragedy was to cart the laundry elsewhere. It was easier to carry clothes – wet or dry – than it was to carry water. As the washing of prints required a good deal of water, the next thing we would have to do is to move the darkroom from the smallholding to the studio in town where there was municipal water. (So much for being at home with the kids!). We hoped that the meagre supply left in the tanks would then last for drinking, cooking and bathing until the rains came.

Tim and I pasted aluminium foil over the windows of the bathroom at the studio to create a temporary darkroom, and brought over a minimum of equipment to get it operative. At about this time, I had purchased an old washing machine with hand wringers for ten rand. This was installed in the darkroom-cum-bathroom, where I did the family washing several times per week. Usually I would tackle this chore before opening in the morning, or after closing in the evening.

One morning my little black maid, Tamara put a particularly full laundry basket in my car. I carried it to the bathroom, dumped it there, and got on with some pressing photographic work. That morning proved to be very busy. I found it demanding attending to the whims of the public, explaining away photographic problems, faults and technicalities that were prevalent, often impeding the service that we would like to have been better. The day positively boomeranged with the unexpected. By late afternoon I was tired, and my surroundings seemed to be cloaked in a mantle of gloom. At five o'clock I pressed the total key on the till. The figure did not compensate for the volume of work done that day. It was disproportionate to the cost of keeping our doors open for a day. I was shocked to calculate that it was actually only twenty five per cent of our average daily running costs!

It was the seventeenth of August. The eighteenth was one day away! That was the date on which number five of the mortgage instalment cheques was due; and not number five only, but number four as well, which, having been returned by our bank as unpaid, was now going to be presented. Where was the money for a double instalment to come from? For some time we had been looking at every possible channel to try and get money in to meet these cheques. However, there had not even been a slight boost in turnover as a token toward the amount required.........

I unloaded the film from the studio camera, and gathered together the orders that had to be printed that night. Tim had been out taking photographs most of the day. I knew that he would come to the studio later that night to develop the films we had exposed that day, in order that we could come in early the following morning to make the prints before the start of the day's business. Licence and passport photographs were always offered for the next day, and one could be sure that the very ones that were not ready promptly would be the ones that were requested early.

I was very tired and looked forward to getting home as soon as possible. I grabbed my handbag, cast my eyes around to check that lights were switched off, and that I had not forgotten anything, and stepped out of the door of the suite. I was about to lock the door when I remembered......... the basket of laundry!

There was nothing for it. It *had* to be done! Otherwise there would not be socks for my husband or school clothes for the children in time. I gritted my teeth and sighed a very deep sigh.........

I thought about my children. This was the time of day that I should be with them. I knew they needed me most as the day turned into night. I could feel their distress. They needed help, not only with their homework, but all their little personal needs. This was the time of day when their difficulties were magnified as they grew tired. I should be there for them! Would my little maid, Tamara be able to cope? Would she have been able to turn out an edible supper? A shudder ran through my body – the involuntary reaction to questions that did not have answers. Stoically, I turned to face the washing.

The machine was of the most primitive, basic design: an open, top-loading tub, which had to be filled with a hand held piece of hose. All the tub had to distinguish it from any ordinary container was that it was fitted with an electrically driven plastic cog in its base, capable of churning a limited quantity of clothes. The clothes, once washed, which was an arbitrary process, had to be lifted out by hand and fed through a two rollers about fifteen inches long that were mounted above the open tub. The rollers had to be turned with a handle – a most laborious, messy process.

Wet clothes were being churned in soap suds in the noisy, old machine; wet clothes were heaped high on the adjacent draining board; wet clothes lay in a bath of rinse water. I had rolled up my sleeves, and valiantly fed the heftier items through the worn rollers. Time ground on. I worked as quickly as I could, and eventually I got to the point where I said to myself "only one more load, and then I'm through with the washing; after that there's only the rinsing........."

My thoughts were disturbed by a loud tap-tap-tap on the door. I heard a deep voice.

"Hi!"

Only one voice could say so little and yet convey so much sarcasm. That sound had rolled off the lips of Dick Shafer. Dick and his wife, Jenny shared the office suite next to ours. They were a couple without children, and they often worked late. There was a reasonably good, if worldly bond of friendship between us; and Tim and I enjoyed Dick's 'hail fellow, well met' personality. However, Jenny was another story. We tolerated her when we did not ignore her. She was one of those young people who no doubt had got into the 'standard seven practical' stream at school, because she was unable to master the academics. Neither had she ever mastered social graces. I think that Lucy had a higher IQ than her.

"Hi!" I called back over the drone of the washing machine.

"Fine time of the day to start work!" Dick's deep voice mocked a serious tone.

I raised my eyes from the piles of washing as he and his wife popped their heads around the bathroom door. What he had actually said was very funny. However, I was so lost in abjection that I could not think of a counter comment. Viciously I ground a sheet through the wringers, as if to endorse my emotion.......... "Starting the day's work, indeed!"

Jenny looked at me aghast. Haven't you even got a *spin dryer?*"

There was no tact in the question, no diplomacy, no sophistication, no guile. She had spoken unashamedly, as out of the mouth of a child. "*You haven't got a spin dryer*" – the statement stripped me of all my cunning. If I had had no answer to her husband's jest, what answer would I have to her naïveté?

Should I answer, "No", and admit that I was defeated by life? Should I answer "Yes", and lie? Could I bear the shame of remaining silent because I was too embarrassed to answer? A hot flush of angry blood rose from my neck to my cheeks. Jenny, of course, despite her IQ, had her home decked with the latest white appliances!

I pretended that my answer had been drowned by the noise of the machine, then I shouted back, as if all was well with me: "Goodnight! See you tomorrow!"

As they left, I realized that I was breaking.

Jenny's question marked the moment in time at which I, Charmazelle Bryant, cracked.

I left the washing in the machine, on the draining board, and in the bath; and made my way through the silent doors of our suite on the first floor of the old building into the foyer above the staircase. The place felt ghost-inhabited when one was alone after dark. Beneath my feet, I felt the soft, mottled blue and purple carpet which Tim and I had had fitted recently to the foyer and staircase in an endeavour to upgrade the place. I made my way down one or two stairs, and sank down there. My face was on my knees; my arms enfolded the calves of my bent up legs, and shortly I felt wetness on my knees, as the tears streamed from my eyes, and rolled down to wet the carpet of royal colours. The floodgates of my soul were opened – there was no end to the troubled waters.

The waters were embittered by failure. My thoughts came like the bullets from an automatic rifle, "You have failed, failed, failed........."

The opaque fumes of gun-smoke were all around me. The stairwell was eerie with the darkness of the cosmos. An accusing spirit came to harass me: "You used to be clever. You were the cleverest in the family. You had wealth, horses, motor cars, position, a profession. You were beautiful too: the world was at your feet when you were eighteen. You could have made it to the top......... Now look at you! Doing a char's job! A lousy, miserable char's job – wringing out the washing by hand. You're in the gutter! Not only haven't you got a spin dryer, but you haven't got a snowball's hope in hell of getting a spin dryer........."

"*Spin dryer*! Ha, ha, ha." I laughed. If I had to sit down and write a list of the things I need, 'spin dryer' would not even feature in the first hundred items. What an idiot Jenny is, but she's got a spin dryer!"

I ground my teeth and grabbed at the air with desperate hands, wailing into the dark, empty building: "*I've got no bloody spin dryer!*"

The powers of darkness were all around me. The onslaught of despair impaired my mind. I became suicidal. Was the pain I felt self accusation or autosuggestion, or was some special emissary of the night sent to torment me?

"What are you doing here? What ignoble end have you reached? What failure is your portion? You should have known when you married Tim. You should have known there would be no spin dryer. You should have known, you should have known………." The accuser fired silent, agonizing words at me.

I had no fear of being alone in the multi-storey, uninhabited, dark building; the fear I had was of another dimension. I had agonized until my emotions were numb. The questions, *what now, what next* were unanswerable. I wept, and wept again. Then the remorse took the form of a spirit of bitterness; the thought came suddenly, sent like a bat from a dark, dank, distant place on a radar course to bomb my overwrought mind.

"Tim, its Tim's fault!"

I identified the substance of a new emotion: hatred. That's what it was: hatred – hatred for Tim!

Bitterness and hatred were fuel for the fire of hopelessness. Time went by in that eerie place. I was isolated, but not alone. Spirits of the dead were there, spectres haunting the scene of past transgressions, mortifying the present despair.

"*Spin dryer………*" The night wolves howled from the recesses of hell.

EIGHT

THE BAPTISM IN JESUS' NAME

The twentieth of August was a tranquil, clear, spring morning. Rob telephoned Tim early that day.

"There is a holiday cottage, not three kilometres from your farm. Members of the body in Pietermaritzburg are holidaying there. You would be welcome for lunch. We will be getting there at about ten. Bring the family – the cottage is right on a swimming beach.

"That would be grand!" Tim said.

Quietly, stoically I gathered children and swimming gear together for a Sunday out. I resolved that I would get through the day by saying little and feeling nothing. I intended to remain insentient, impassive and aloof. No words need to be spoken, no one would know......... that the Bryants were going bankrupt; that they had no water at home; no spin dryer to cope with the laundry after work; and that my life was embittered by the knowledge that I was a failure. I resolved to keep the matter silent.

However, when we arrived at the beach cottage, I was overwhelmed by Christian love. We were made to feel so welcome. There was a most precious attitude of caring and unity. This is what tempered my hardness of heart; what broke my resolute decision of silence. I was softened to a point where I knew that it was not possible to maintain the uncommunicative stance I had vowed to adopt.

When the outer shell cracked, it released a flow of tears from deep within. These tears were not only tears of hurt, fear, grief and loss, but tears of repentance too, and the tears were the beginning of a process of inner healing.

All that day I sat back in an easy chair, a little apart from the circle of people, and I wept. They worshipped God, they broke bread, they sang praises, and exchanged testimonies – while my tears continued to flow. The beauty of the situation was that I was free to shed my tears without any intrusion; no probing questions, no psycho-analysis; no transgression of social etiquette, because the believers were people who moved in the Spirit, and they were aware that the Holy Spirit was doing a work in me.

Rob, meanwhile, had been explaining to Tim about foundations. A wisp of a phrase here and there registered in my consciousness. I heard "… buried with Jesus", and "… in Jesus' name". I gave little heed to the gist of what he was trying to impart.

Before we left that evening, a bond of sisterly love had been established between our hostess, Esther Wood and I. Esther was an older, motherly woman – no doubt a person used by the Lord to comfort the tears of those in need. She was indeed some-one I could love, trust and confide in.

It happened then, that when, on the following Thursday, a letter arrived from our bondholder's attorneys demanding repayment of the entire loan with costs and interest, it was to Esther that I ran, to share with her the first traumatic news of the shock.

Esther came out to greet me when she heard my car arrive.

"Charmazelle!" She cried.

"Esther!" My palate was so dry I could hardly speak, but I managed the agonized whisper: "They have called up our bond!"

She extended both arms to me. "Well, praise the Lord!" She said

My answer, "I can't" was buried in our embrace.

Esther remained silent as she held me, waiting on the Lord for words of guidance.

"What makes it all the more heart rending, is that I received the letter today. It is my birthday........."

"Well, happy birthday!" She cried

Even in my extreme state of stress, I knew that Esther knew that God was working it all out to the good of those who love him; but I could not receive this consolation.

Esther took my temples in both hands, and looked at me with *agape* love – the love of God that transcends human emotion. That look of love embodied peace, such as only Jesus can give – peace that surpasses human understanding........

I saw the peace – a spiritual realm that can be entered into, that was there for the taking; but I knew that I was not yet ready to come into it. It was not yet the time to quench the fever raging in my ailing soul.

*   *   *

That evening Tim submitted the matter to Rob on the telephone.

"I have received a letter from my bondholders."

"Hmmmm." As only Rob could conjecture.

"This is a point of submission. They want the whole capital amount paid by the end of the month. What should I do?"

"Nothing." Rob's tone was unemotional.

Tim contemplated his answer for a moment in silence, and when the understanding dawned, he said: "I see."

My reaction to the conversation that Tim related to me was anger!

Tim tried to give me reason: "We are God's responsibility."

This concept was absolutely foreign to my intellect, and I rejected it as absurd. Surely, this was the time to take the world into our hands, as though it had two handles, and shake these handles violently until somebody noticed or something happened. Surely it was a time to cry *'help'* with a voice that would rend the heavens. There must be some form of negotiation that could be done. Surely there was a buyer somewhere out there in the sea of economic recession, who would help us with an outright purchase of the place. I implored God for a buyer. Every motor car engine that I heard, every ring of the phone that broke the silence, every rap on the door, in fact, any sound that could herald a buyer fired hope in my breast. However, each flicker of hope was extinguished by cold disappointment.

*   *   *

Lighting played among the dark, moving water vapour masses in the sky. Thunder cracked. Storm clouds were pregnant with their heavy load. It was Sunday afternoon, the third of September. We were at the beach cottage again. Our hosts, Esther and her husband were there, Rob and Dalene were there, as well as a group of several other believers. The occasion was that Tim had arranged with Rob to baptize him in the name of Jesus. Whatever it was in scriptures that Rob had pointed out to Tim, had convinced him that this was the right course of action to take.

Our party moved from the cottage, out over the lawns that stretched towards the beach, onto the beach sands towards the waters. The sea was whipped by a high wind. Sand lashed our bare legs. Waves broke with rapidity one after the other. The tide was high, and the sands shelved sharply into the waters. The backwash looked frightening. We ran along the beach passing a rocky outcrop, looking for a place where it would be easier to access the water.

Over the sound of the wind, knowing the others were not in hearing, I cried as I ran, '*I am shaking the dust from my feet*', however I questioned whether my cry was of faith. Would this statement of positive confession have an effectual, authentic impact, or was it only a vain attempt at declaring that I was leaving a world of bondage and lack for a land of promise and plenty – an attempt that would fail?

Rob had had many years of service as a scoutmaster, and knew much about safety, camping out, and the ethic of the Boy Scout movement. In a manner true to the training they propound, he had thought of safety and had brought a rope. Esther's husband held firmly onto the one end of the rope, and Rob took the other end into the sea, while Tim followed him. The two men spoke as the dark water swirled around them. The group on the shore could not hear above the wind. Tim went over backwards on Rob's arm. Rob's words, "In Jesus Name", may have been unheard by the human witnesses, but, as I was to learn, they were heard in the heavenlies.

As Tim came out of the water, I went in. I had been too dazed by emotional suffering to question the whole matter. I was just going to do it. I knew that Rob had given Tim scriptural references as to why one should be baptized in the name of Jesus; and if Tim was going to do it, I would too. As I made my way into the surf, I had no fear of the waves and the rough sea, for I knew it was a course that I must take.

Rob repeated the counselling he had given to Tim, and I vaguely registered the words: "… therefore we are buried with Him", but it was as though I was only semi-cognizant of my situation. He pushed me over backwards, into and under the water, and I came up, surrounded by the rough, grey sea.

I remember the feel of the sand whipping my legs that day on the beach, and the feel of my feet coated with wet sand. The thought that the scripture went on from *'shake off the dust from your feet?'* to another dimension was forming in my mind: yes, indeed I realized I will visit cities, and bring this message, and the message will be to those who do not heed my words, *as a testimony against them!*

Tim had come out of the waters a new man. Fear, insecurity and lack of self confidence, attitudes with long standing footholds in his life, were suddenly dispelled. He gained an inner peace from the experience in turbulent waters. He no longer feared any man! His face changed and his voice changed; he developed a trust in God that gave him purposeful new confidence. He was no longer dragged down by the fact that our bond had been called up. He was endowed with supernatural strength – albeit that he would need it to face the refining fire of the next few months.

I loved Tim! I was proud of his new, positive attitude, and I repented of my thoughts of hatred toward him during the emotional havoc I had recently endured. While pondering over the amazing changes in my husband, I discerned a more profound meaning to our recent baptism.

Although the experience appeared to have no physical or emotional impact on me at the time, there was unseen victory in the spirit. I had been through financial stress, physical stress, and had lived in fear of losing our assets and means of livelihood; which still loomed as a daily threat. Nevertheless, drugged by heartache as I was, I was willing to submit to the *type* of burial, although I could not for a moment understand why our original baptism in the name of the Father, the Son and the Holy Spirit did not suffice.

There was a time lapse between that which was initiated in the spirit, and that which was to be performed in the actual. I had been fighting, fighting, fighting the logic of the act, yet willing to submit at the time. I had done my part. I had gone into the waters. Henceforth the Lord would be fighting for me. For some time I remained dumb about the need for baptism in Jesus' name, and then on a visit to the Knight's home at a later date, I asked Rob:

"Why does one have to be baptized in Jesus' name?'

"It's very simple," he said, "There is one scripture, Mathew twenty eight, verse nineteen that refers to baptism into the name of the Father, the Son and the Holy Ghost, written *before* the ascension, *before* Jesus was glorified."

Tim held my hand while we listened.

"*After* Jesus rose to be seated in glory on the right hand of the Father, all the scriptures that were written, starting with Acts chapter two, verse thirty eight – have a look at a concordance to get the list – speak of baptism into Jesus' name. We have to be buried with Him in baptism." Rob picked up a bible, then continued, "Here, in Romans chapter six......" he said opening the page:

> "Or do you not know that as many of us as were baptized into Christ Jesus were baptized into His death?
>
> Therefore we were buried with Him through baptism into death, that just as Christ was raised from the dead by the glory of the Father, even so we should also walk in newness of life."
>
> Romans 6:3-4

To walk in newness of life, I realized, would mean that I could give up battling, for henceforth the Lord would be fighting for me.

*   *   *

Days turned into weeks, and my anxiety about saving our property increased. The war of contradiction still raged in my mind. Tim rested in the assurance that we should continue to 'do nothing' about our property that was in jeopardy. In many ways his calm confidence was fuel for the fire of my restlessness. Where-as he was peacefully trusting God for a miracle with our finances, I was up and about, determined to *do something*. Tim had established that the wheels of the law wound in slow motion, and it would take several months for our property to be attached and sold under writ of execution, but some of those months had already passed, and I was beset by the frantic urgency of the affair.

"Can we not advertise?" I cried.

"Yes. We can advertise." Tim said.

My spirit rose at his affirmative statement.

"Where would you like to place adverts?" He asked.

I knew that he was trying to appease me, but I was determined not to lose hope. I mentioned the names of several publications. Later that day I wrote out the adverts and we posted them off, together with the fees – precious money that we could ill afford to lose at the time.........

I might have known from the onset that those ads would not meet their mark. It was too fond a hope to be clung to on the grindstone of reality. There must, however, be an option other than to '*do nothing*'

I contemplated the phenomenon of submission, but constantly refuted the idea as impractical. To do nothing would be an act of submission that would take more courage on my behalf than, figuratively, to turn the world upside down doing *something*!

NINE

THE GATEKEEPER

I was in the studio one morning when the telephone rang.

A cultured, commanding voice came over the line. "Is that the photographers?"

"Yes. This is Charmazelle Bryant speaking."

"Oh, good morning! This is Mrs. Lang. I am the convener of the Women's Institute Flower Show. Our annual show is being held in the town hall, starting next Thursday. Now, we will want some photographs!"

"Oh, yes!"

"There is to be an official opening by the Mayoress, and, naturally we will want photos for the press. We will also need photos of the prize-winning entries for our records, and I should imagine the exhibitors themselves will want copies."

I asked Mrs. Lang for a few further details, and thanked her for calling. I was very pleased to have been asked to do the job, as normally the local newspaper was asked, and we missed out on this type of business. This was an important commission, and I considered it something of a breakthrough, in addition to being an event that would boost our turnover.

Thursday came. I checked my equipment bag, and saw to it that I was at the town hall in good time.

All the right people were there: with a few glances I picked out the important ladies of the town. The stronghold of the local social elite was more than adequately represented – this was a place to be seen at. The official opening of the flower show was conducted with the expected pomp and ceremony, and a list of charities that the event supported was read out.

I took the necessary photographs during the proceedings, and afterwards drank in the beauty of many of the original flower arrangements, marvelling at many of the exotic blooms, while photographing the individual exhibits. Before leaving, I went to thank Mrs. Lang for asking me, and bid her goodbye.

The convener was an outspoken lady: "Those press photographs will be needed to meet the paper's deadline at nine o'clock tomorrow morning!" Her attitude conveyed the words, 'just you see to it that you don't let us down!'

Back at the studio, I snatched a sandwich and a cup of tea for lunch, only to be interrupted by the telephone. It was Tim.

"The Sugar Mill want routine maintenance photographs taken this afternoon. It might be quite a long, drawn-out affair, because I'll have to follow the fitters up as they dismantle certain of the plant. I don't think I'll be through before five."

"Well, shall I develop the films after work? That'll save you a trip back into town." I said this as our smallholding was situated out beyond the Mill.

"If you feel confident about doing it." Tim said.

Although I had done a lot of printing, I had only developed film on one or two occasions. This was a sensitive procedure, which Tim always performed, as he had had years of experience before I came into photography. However, I felt confident enough to say, "I should manage."

"The developing time is fifteen minutes with the chemical I have mixed. Don't forget to turn the developing can a hundred and eighty degrees, every minute exactly."

"Okay." I was however, a little worried about loading the film from the cassettes onto the developing reels. "Hope I can get the film in smoothly."

"Please be careful of dust and finger prints!" Film was sacred material to Tim.

Once I had closed the doors of the studio to the public at five, I made my way to the darkroom. I sighed, and I cursed the drought! We could not start developing film before five, because of the risk of interruption from the public at a crucial stage of the developing. It was so much easier to do the work after hours at home, instead of having to stay on in an evacuated town after dark, while worrying about young children who needed care. I closed the darkroom door behind me. There seemed to be an unusually bright vertical line of light between the door and the frame. Doubt arose in my mind as to whether this strip of light was sufficient to harm the film. This doubt made me nervous at the onset of the process. Should I take the film out or not? There was little I could do about the strip of light. I decided to take the chance, but this made my normally steady hands shake as I worked. I started to wind the first film out of the cassette onto the developing reel. It wouldn't take and slide in! I strove to rectify it, but still it wouldn't take. No matter how I forced or persuaded, the film would not go in! This, of course, diminished the little bit of composure I had about the crack of light. In my struggle I wound more and more film out of the cassette, no doubt exposing it to more light than it would have had if it had wound smoothly into the light-tight developing reel. Eventually the cassette swung from the end of the metre long (thirty five millimetre) film strip. I knew what finger prints would do to the undeveloped cellulose, however I had no option but to handle the film again and again, while I entertained horrible visions of the photos of the faces of the snottiest customers being marred! I started to sweat. Tim would have been horrified at the lack of respect shown to the film. I was almost in tears, more particularly as we could not afford the loss.

Finally, the film took. As I slid it deeper into the reel, I could not understand what had jammed it in the first place. When the two films were loaded, it was with much relief that I switched on the light. Then I started with the chemicals. It was simple enough. Tim had made his own labels for the dark glass bottles. It was quite straightforward and easy to understand. I reached for the first bottle and poured it into the film developing drum. Then I spent fifteen minutes agitating meticulously.

It was growing dark outside. The place was eerie, because of the vastness of the building, deserted by all, except me. I shivered, and shrugged off a fear of the place. Thank goodness Tim would be with the children by now, so I did not have to worry about them!

At last the developing was finished. I connected the drum to the water tap and rinsed it out. Then I reached for the canister of fixer. As I clutched the container, I felt the same primaeval instinct for survival that the deer feels at the water hole when it knows that the predator has singled it out, and was about to plunge.

The lid of the fixer bottle was wet!

I tried to remember......... I strove to recollect the logical sequence of events. What were my actions some twenty minutes ago? How did that lid get wet if I had not handled the container?

'Have I used the wrong chemicals first?' The thought rasped my mind.

It was impossible for me to remember! Here, then, was a cause of deep concern of another kind: was I experiencing memory loss as an aftermath of stress? Was my brain chemistry whacky? Had high levels of the stress hormone, cortisol affected the neurotransmitters in my brain? These frightening possibilities were part and parcel of the maelstrom of events that broke me.

I poured the fixer into the developing drum anyway, and carried on with the fixing process for the specified period of time, continuing, however thin the thread of hope, until the alarm rang. Then I opened the drum and extracted the first film.

It was clear! Transparent – totally wiped out!

There was not an image on either of the films! This represented a loss of two days turnover – two good days, as we had had more work than usual. The greater loss was that of the photographs of the flower show – those, of course, were irreplaceable! For the rest, we would have to face each and every customer, recite our tale of woe, and retake all the routine studio shots. But what of Mrs. Lang? How would we explain the catastrophe to her? And what good would excuses be, anyway? Reputation and reliability were vital to our image as photographers – the talk would be right round the town!

I left the dark, lonely building.

The rural area beyond the town was deserted; the lights of my little car forged an uncertain pathway into the blanket of night. I wept as I steered into the blackness, following the country road that wound through sugar cane lands leading to our little home.

On arriving home I told Tim about the dreadful mistake I had made. *"How could I have done it?"*

"Easily. You just made a mistake with the chemicals. You are not used to that work."

"I feel defeated. I am a miserable failure."

"There is no condemnation........."

I didn't want to hear scripture. I interrupted, "I couldn't face the people. I couldn't face anything, anymore in this town! I am quite beyond the point going back to mop up the mess!"

Tim was a man of few words. He listened with patience and understanding.

I grappled with words to continue. "I'm finished. I have......... had......... just about all I take. I can think of a hundred clichés, the end of the line, the last straw, over the edge, but Timothy, now I really mean it – I cannot carry on!"

The tears welled in Tim's eyes. He felt responsible for me, his wife, and hated to see me broken. He knew that I knew that he would have avoided this situation if he could have. He had tried – tried, expecting the outcome to be otherwise. The road had been rough......... He did not speak, lest he say something in his own understanding that would hurt. In all this turmoil, there was an unexplained confidence in him, which I could not help being aware of. I knew that he knew that God was working in the situation, despite the fact that I did not want to hear this.

I was trying to justify my breakdown in lieu of the recent chain of events. It was not only the big things like the washing machine episode, and losing Mrs. Lang's pictures, it was the myriads of little things – the daily buffeting caused by lack of water at home, and lack of capital at work. We were continually unable to let customers have work on time, because we were continually short of raw materials to do the job. This, in turn, had its effect on cash flow, and we were caught in the riptide.

This tide had now swept me to a place from which I could not return. I was, as it were, fast approaching an outcrop of rock, upon which the waters broke with fury. Accelerating toward destruction, I blacked out; reaching a state of mental inertia beyond caring, beyond emotional suffering, beyond any sense of responsibility. I did not return to the studio – just left it to Tim; left it, with the knowledge that the business needed me, but helpless to assuage the situation. The blank immobility of my mind continued for many days, and then a chain of thoughts came to harass me time and again:

"Do nothing." Why had Rob said, *do nothing?* But why did Tim submit to this suggestion? Surely somebody could do *something!*

I felt far from God; rejected, separated. My relationship with Jesus and with my heavenly Father was at all time low, steeped as I was in hopelessness. I neither sought for, nor expected any miracle. My belief was that all was going to be lost, and I had better grin and bear it.

*   *   *

It happened that one of my front teeth broke off close to the gum, and it became something of an emergency to get a dentist's appointment.

After an examination of my top teeth the dentist said: "The only way we can close the gap is with a bridge."

"What does that involve?" I asked, thinking not of the pain or the discomfort, but of the cost.

"We will have to crown the teeth on either side, and bring a bridge across. Only two appointments will be necessary. However, with this type of work we require a fifty per cent deposit as the bridge has to be especially made."

"And what will it cost?"

"Two hundred and fifty rand."

"I see." What I saw was that the situation was impossible. I couldn't be seen with the broken tooth, and I had no idea of how to pay for the alternative.

Later on that evening when I was alone with Tim, I told him that I needed a hundred and twenty five rand for the dentist's deposit, knowing full well that he did not have the money.

He simply lifted his eyes heavenward, and said, "Father my wife needs a hundred and twenty five rand for a new tooth."

*   *   *

A handful of believers were gathered at the Knight's home one Sunday. Dalene sat at the piano.

Some-one asked: "Would you play the Psalm 61 music?"

The presence of the Lord was in that place, as the notes of the melody pealed forth, and people raised their voices, singing in unison to worship God:

> *"Hear my cry, O God,*
> *Attend unto my prayer.*
> *From the end of the earth will I cry unto thee.*
> *When my heart is overwhelmed:*
> *Lead me to the Rock,*
> *That is higher than I,*
> *That is higher than I"*

Psalm 61:1-2 Authorised KJV (italics mine)
(last line repeated for the gospel chorus)

'Damn it!' I thought. 'I get through the days by gritting my teeth and switching off. Then I can hold my emotions at bay, without cracking or screaming or going off the rails. Now, I hear this music and my heart wants to break! Like that day at the beach cottage, when I was quite resolved to maintain my stoical stance, but the love of the Christians broke through the ramparts, and drew me out from the dark cul-de-sac I was in.'

Dalene played the tune again. The words and the melody rang through my heart and mind, finding, as it were, another person behind the façade – a living being behind the armour.

The thought came to me that God loved me. 'No Lord, don't convict me of the thought that You love me. I have no tears left for my remorse. Leave me with the dryness of my soul; leave me in the void of emptiness and silence that accompanies my hurt and fear.' I did not want to be a part of the love and joy and worship, because I knew that I could not enter into that realm. Mine was a realm of suffering that they did not understand.

Rob had purposed that they would break bread that evening. Different people prayed as the Spirit led. As God would have it, there was a lady, a newly baptised Christian, sitting to the right of me. She knew nothing about me at all. At a time when it seemed that everyone who had wanted to pray, had prayed; and all that had to be said had been said, the lady next to me spoke:

"My sister, there is some matter in which the Lord has not yet undertaken for you."

"Yes........." I answered faintly.

"May we pray for you?" She asked sincerely.

I indicated in the affirmative.

They prayed.

Rob had his cue. He rose and came directly over to me. Tim followed him and the two men kneeled together in front of my chair.

Rob always had authority in spiritual warfare: "Satan, I command you, in the name of Jesus, to leave this woman alone!"

I trembled and started praying aloud in tongues.

"Don't pray in tongues. Just keep quiet and let it come out." Rob said.

I obeyed. I tried to make my mouth and my mind an open channel. I had no idea what to expect. How would the demon come out? What would I feel? I was nervous, apprehensive and embarrassed to say the least.

"I come against you with the blood of the Lamb!" Rob said, addressing not me, but that which was within me.

I desperately wanted to co-operate but my every thought and attempt seemed futile.

Rob continued to rebuke the spirit. "The blood of Jesus is against you!"

Both Tim and Rob continued to repeat this injunction, while others in the circle prayed.

Eventually I began to think that the whole thing was hopeless. Nothing was going to happen. We were wasting our time. After repeated commands to the spirit to get it to move, without result, the men resumed their seats. I felt weak and limp and sleepy. I opened the doors of my mind again to the dream world of gnarled trees and dark shadows, and I knew that I was beckoned by an eerie presence that blended with the darkness. There was an ominous welcome in the rustle of many leaves, a carpet underfoot, dank and soft, prepared over many seasons. I answered the call and went in. The doors closed behind me, and I was no longer with the Christians in the Knight's living room.

Meanwhile Rob was blessing bread and wine, and began to pass it round.

Although I was with the believers in body, I was not with them in mind. I escaped again via a schizophrenic episode down the shadowy paths of catastrophe.

However, after a while, I forced myself to come to; I was here, in the Knight's lounge, sitting in a circle of people who loved me. The dividing line between who I was, and who I was supposed to become, was undefined – lost in an illusionary haze.

The plate with the unleavened bread, symbolic of the body of Christ was passed around. I took a piece and lifted it to my mouth to eat. Then I hesitated. Was there an excuse for performing an act without being capable of making a decision? This was a serious matter. I *had* to make a decision.........

The decision I had to make was to forgive – to forgive unconditionally, as I had been forgiven. But who? Who to forgive? And, if I could think of who, then what, and how? "God help me to forgive........."

I placed the bread in my mouth, and slowly started to eat, in faith that God would help me, as I could not help myself.

Rob was reading: "This cup is the new covenant in My blood, which is shed for you."

Luke 22:20

The cup was passed from person to person in silence, and each drank before passing it on. Then came my turn: I put the goblet to my lips, but could not drink. A mighty battle raged in the spirit. I started fighting against what was happening.........

I had to use every bit of will power that I could muster in order to overcome the embarrassment that I thought I would feel. It seemed a superhuman act of will to open my mouth! I was frightened of the humiliation. I was striving, battling to deal with this sudden fear. And then it could no longer be held......... as lightning flashes from east to the west with blinding rapidity, so an ear-shattering screech flashed from my mouth, and appeared to hit the ceiling of the room, as an explosion within the room would do. The room reverberated with the infernal sound.

I could not believe that I had made that sound; but I knew that whatever it was, that thing had to be given vent to, before I could drink from the cup that symbolized the blood of Jesus!

Everyone was crying, "Halleluiah!" They were praising God with one voice.

After a while, Rob said: "That was the gate-keeper!"

'Gate-keeper,' I thought, 'Then, that means there are more! Impossible! That loud scream was everything!'

So often Rob said things that I did not want to hear.

TEN

TO PREPARE ME FOR MY BURIAL

On the day following the gatekeeper episode, Tim arrived home excited. He had a testimony and lost no time in telling me: "The money has arrived for your tooth!"

I was querulous, "Really?"

"I was out of the studio for a while about midday, and while I was away somebody brought a bulging envelope and gave it to the maid, telling her to give it to me. The envelope wasn't even properly sealed, and in fact, I just found it lying on my desk."

"That's amazing. Praise the Lord!" I cried. "Who sent the money?"

"There was a note inside, here I'll read it: 'The Lord told me that you have need of this.' It is unsigned. I have counted the notes. There is two hundred and fifty rand. Praise God! He is so good!"

This episode is one of the many small areas of light that shone forth during the dark period of my life before the great and wonderful spiritual release that I was to experience.

I made the necessary appointments with the dentist, and once the bridge had been fitted, I ran my tongue over it, feeling it smooth but foreign in my mouth.

A witness of the Lord speaking to me from within was heard: "This is the covenant of My provision for you. The reminder is very close to you, even in your mouth, where you are often conscious of it, and you will know that you cannot be far from My care." I was much uplifted by this sign from God, and was deeply thankful to Him for this evidence of His care for me.

Spring matured into early summer, and the month of October heralded rain! This brought water into our tanks, and we were able to move the darkroom back to our home. I continued to do quite a lot of the printing during the day.

Although there were many small evidences of God's love for us, often expressed through believers in the body of Christ, I still found it difficult to be at peace. I knew that something still had to *happen* to bring me closer to God. At times I agonised in my mind over the situation. What caused the sense of separation, why was my outlook misted by uneasiness, and how could the breach be mended? What was wrong between God and I?

One day, Tim and I sat down together at home, and I tried to express my thoughts, hoping to expose the root cause of the state of uneasiness I had had since being saved. The words I used to describe my feelings to Tim, seemed absolutely inadequate: "I haven't arrived. I've missed something."

"What did Jesus do when he came into the temple, and found that His Father's house was being used as a house of merchandise?" Tim asked in a gentle tone.

"He was angry with the people. He kicked them out." I replied.

"Yes, He made a whip of cords, and drove the animals out, and overturned the tables of the moneychangers."

I visualized the outer court of the temple turned into a filthy market place.

"There was buying and selling and money changing in the outer court. It was not a fit place to enclose the sanctuary where God dwells."

"No." I agreed.

"We are spirit, soul and body, like the three parts of the temple."

"And the filthy market place needs to be swept clean and sanctified?"

"That's right." Tim nodded in affirmation.

I had to acknowledge that it was a very interesting point – there was, in fact, excitement in the spiritual truth, albeit that it was hard for me to accept. However, I knew that I had to accept it if I was to grow, and be healed, and be at peace with God. Could I admit, even to myself, that my body was the outer court, and that it was defiled by filthy merchandise? What a simile! My soul, which should be part of the temple of the Lord, was nothing but a market place. I was not glorifying God in my mind, I was working out finances – day and night. It was just finance, finance, finance. I had to make the decision to drive out the moneychangers, that my mind and body may be a place fit for the Holy Spirit to dwell.

During that month of October, my body cracked. I suffered the most severe dose of bronchitis ever. My lungs ached with every breath that I took. My body was racked with a high fever. Sleep was fitful, and it was horrible to waken to the awareness of my sore throat and chest, dry mouth and nasal passages blocked with phlegm. The antibiotic that I took was slow acting, and only after many days did I start to make a gradual recovery.

After the illness, I was overcome by crushing depression. I could not think about God – I felt utterly separated from Him. I could only think about my defeat: I had failed as a mother, I had failed as a wife, I had failed as a business partner. Again I walked the darkened avenue beneath the rustling leaves of canopying trees – leaves that were ever whispering to me, courting me, inviting me into their world. Just one leap from the world of the actual, and I would be in the world of the unreal. Suicide was a very attractive option.........

As the bronchitis eased out of my system, another disease took over – insomnia! Night after agonizing night I was unable to sleep. The pain of exhaustion increased day after day, despite the fact that I thought it could not get worse. The relentless horror of the long, dark nights haunted me. It was impossible to switch off and enter into the state of oblivion I so badly needed; it was frustrating not to have the control over my mind to close it down and enter the dream world I needed. Day after day I lay on the bed too exhausted to want to do anything, and night after night the battle would rage in my conscious thoughts denying me the sleep I was trying to get.

One morning, as I lay on the bed, I reached for a bible from my bedside table. I moved to prop myself up on pillows, and the bible fell open. I looked down at the book: the page was open at Romans, chapter twelve, and I started reading from verse one:

> "I beseech you therefore, brethren, by the mercies of God,
> that *you present your bodies a living sacrifice*, holy, acceptable
> unto God, which is your reasonable service."

Romans 12:1 (italics mine)

"What a thought!" I said aloud. "A sacrifice! To God!" I pondered over the impact of the words, which the Holy Spirit had emboldened in italics: *present your bodies a living sacrifice.........*

To my way of thinking, the concept of sacrifice belonged to black magic, and the very word sacrifice had always been rather ugly. In modern times, people didn't make sacrifices! That surely, was an ancient rite – some obscure practice of the old-testament days. To bring the concept of sacrifice into my life as it was being lived in the present day and age, seemed absurd and unacceptable. The traditional religions I had known previously would never even have suggested such a thing! Something in me shied from the very thought of sacrifice, and the resultant visions of blood-guiltiness.

Sacrifice, to me, had meant blood and death, but I began to catch a glimpse of another meaning of the word. To sacrifice yourself to some-one was to give yourself up to do their will, and relinquish your own rights. I contemplated doing God's will all the time, and not my own. The concept that I did not own myself, but was owned as the result of a voluntary sacrifice of myself, began to interest me. It was certainly a very far cry from continually fuelling the wheel of endeavour to make a living and protect our assets. If, for instance, I did not have to worry about myself and my family, because I had surrendered myself, and my rights and ambitions, how would life be? I continued to reflect on that word, *sacrifice*, with its many facets during my illness.

My chest was still very sore, and I had developed a chronic cough after the bronchitis. The sleepless nights had become unbearable, and one morning I realized with conviction that I must do something. I took stock of my situation: What day of the week was it? Thursday. I had better try to rise out of the abyss, and try to resume my role as wife and mother......... What time was it? Nine o'clock. I resolved that I would phone Emily Tarlton, a spirit-filled believer from the Shelley Beach church, and ask her to pray for me.

Emily had been a type of spiritual mother to me since Tim and I were first baptized. Her manner was forthright and positive; and anyone who met her would instinctively know that here was some-one in whom they could place absolute trust. A bond of love developed between us, and Tim and I often attended prayer meetings at her home. Emily was a Christian warrior in the true sense of the word. She was a practical person, who not only read the bible, but did what it says we can do in Jesus' name. People phoned her from far and wide when help was needed. Many a time I had needed prayer for a sick child, and when I phoned her, she would not waste time. She would tell me to hold the telephone receiver as a point of contact, and would immediately lift her voice to rebuke the sickness, and pray for the Holy Spirit to touch the child. I clearly remember a day when little Jill had a high fever. Emily lived near the pre-primary school Jill attended, and Tim and I called on her early one morning on our way to work. We each had a hand on the little one's forehead, and as Emily prayed, I veritably felt Jill's forehead cool down under my touch. The fever left completely and she was fine to go to school.

However, I expected that when I phoned Emily, she would once again ask me to hold the receiver of the phone as a point of contact, and that she would pray for me there and then. I moved toward the telephone, but stopped in my tracks, nervous and uncertain.

"I had better get a scripture from the Lord before 'phoning" I said to myself.

I turned to find a bible. God answered me before I asked, "Matthew twenty six, verse twelve."

> "For when she poured this perfume on my body,
> She did it *to prepare me for burial.*"

> Matthew 26:12 NIV

I was quite startled. Had I got the wrong scripture? But no, I thought, for it was as though the phrase, *prepare me for my burial,* was emboldened in italics.

"BURIAL!" I said almost aloud, "MY BURIAL!"

I went on to think about death. My death? Precious ointment on my body?

There was a quickening within me. I took the courage to say, "Praise God. My body is going to be anointed with precious ointment, because I am going to undergo a type of burial."

I was excited as I remembered a few words of Rob's teaching on baptism. "What is baptism", he would ask, and then patiently answer, "Death, burial and resurrection."

I knew that my recent baptism was a stepping stone of obedience. I had never DIED in the water. My old self with all my heartaches and shortcomings was still there – there was not the fresh fragrance of a newness of life that I had heard about. The hurts and heartaches of the past still had rule in my members; the new blossom could not burst forth in bloom, for it was hampered by past bruises......... I knew that I must phone Emily.

"Goodness, gracious, is that Charmazelle?" Emily's question came through with exclamation.

'Yes."

Her voice was warm and vibrant. "How lovely to hear from you. How are you."

"Oh......... not too good." There was a hint of a tear in my voice. "How are you?"

"I am fine. Praising the Lord!"

"Emily. I......... I think I need prayer."

"You must come and see me." It was as though Emily had been shown the wider picture by the Spirit of God. "Now just you hold on right there. I am going to phone Ruth, and see whether she can meet us here at about 11 o'clock. I will phone you right back."

"Okay." I said. "Bye for now."

As I replaced the receiver it occurred to me that, although Emily's voice had been full of love, there was something uncannily businesslike about her manner. How did she know that she would need spiritual reinforcements?

It was not long before she phoned back: "Charmazelle, it will be fine for eleven. Ruth will be able to come, and Frieda will come too. We'll see you then."

ELEVEN

SHALL I BRING TO THE POINT OF BIRTH AND NOT GIVE DELIVERY?

Emily made me feel most welcome when I arrived at her house. She was a lovely, cheerful person who must have been very beautiful in her day; now she was probably old enough to be my mother. Her skin was unmarked, her complexion good, and her blue-grey eyes were enhanced by symmetrical brows. Her heart-shaped face was topped with abundant brown curls, highlighted by wisps of grey. She had an ample figure, and her body language and gestures made one feel absolutely at home. She brewed a pot of tea, and we chatted while I helped her set cups and saucers on a tray. There were always delicious home-baked eats at Emily's house, and I arranged cookies on a beautiful serving plate. The table was set, and we were quite ready by the time Ruth and Frieda arrived. We greeted one another with hugs; introductions were not necessary as we knew one another from the Shelley Beach church.

Ruth was Emily's special friend, a lady of about the same age, also robust, but with a prominent jaw, and straight, greying hair taken back from her face. She was an outspoken, no-nonsense person, and a great prayer warrior of the congregation. Frieda was a vivacious woman, with a slightly freckled face, and red hair, who made up in personality what she lacked in beauty. She had lovely dark brown eyes set in an oval face, and at first glance her strength of character was evident.

As the conversation progressed from greetings to the business of the day, I was conscious of a supernatural bond of Christian love between us – a bond that was stronger than the bond of normal human affection. It was a love that went beyond the natural, filial love that we felt for one another as sisters in the Lord – it was an agape[1] love which embraced complete trust and total commitment to one another. Little did I know just then how important this love was going to be, for I was about to walk a high, winding pathway flanking a precipice; a pathway paved with loose, chipped stone on which I could easily have dashed a foot and fallen, had I not been braced by the care and Christian love of these ladies.

Ruth addressed Emily: "I would like some pencils and paper."

I started to feel incredibly tired. It was not as a result of the sleepless nights I had suffered – it was a different feeling – a sudden distinct numbing of my senses. The room became clouded as it were, and I was dulled to the awareness of my surroundings. Before I could take stock of the situation, I found the three ladies seated around me. I became alarmed when I noticed them with pencils poised above paper. I knew in a part of me that there was something frightening about to happen, but I knew that happen, it must, for I was semi-anaesthetised and I could not escape. I felt like a patient who had been tranquilized and was lying on a trolley waiting to be wheeled into the operating theatre. I knew that they knew that the time was ripe.........

Ruth was very methodical and began to ask forthright questions without hesitation: "What is the matter?"

"I can't sleep at night. I am so tired my whole body aches." I answered.

---

[1]   The Greek word for a God kind of love.

Emily and Frieda wrote something down. I glanced obliquely at one the notepads, and saw the word "insomnia" heading the list.

"Why can't you sleep at night?"

I sighed audibly. How could I explain? How could these dear housewives, who normally did not deal with business matters, know what it meant to have a bond called up? However, I stated the fact as simply as I could without emphasis or explanation. "We have had our bond called up."

"Oh?" They asked together, and I noticed Ruth's voice was a little higher pitched than before.

Their querulous comment confirmed that they did not have the necessary understanding of the implications involved, and hence the agony it had caused me.

Involuntarily I started one of the coughing fits that had befallen me since my bout of bronchitis. The ladies rallied round me with a box of tissues, and a refuelling of hot tea. While Emily was attending to me I glanced across at Frieda's notepad, and saw the word 'bitterness' following 'insomnia'. For a moment I wondered how I had got into the humiliating situation that I was in. My flesh called for a cigarette to subdue the emotion, but I was too ashamed to light up, because of the coughing fit. What would they say!

"Did you feel like this before.......... the.......... bond was called up?" Ruth asked slowly.

"Well, no, not like this. I've always coped with life before. Tim and I haven't been able to make ends meet in the shop for some time. My nerves are finished, and I have come to a point where I feel I can't cope any more, so I've actually stayed away from the shop and left it to him. But that is not like me, because I know that I am needed there."

They wrote something down.

I grimaced. The psycho-analysis was chaffing me.

"Are you frightened of anything?"

"No." I had always been proud of my courage. People used to tell me I had courage when I was a child; when I was recovering from the motor accident courage had been an important crutch to me.

"What about poverty?"

I was silent for some time. I didn't like the question. It had a bad taste. I didn't in any way want to be associated with *poverty* – that was a different scenario to failed entrepreneurship. "Now that you ask, yes, I suppose, that is a way of putting it. I fear bankruptcy."

I noted the pencils in action: 'poverty', 'fear', and 'hatred' were all on Frieda's list. 'Now they really are making mountains out of molehills', I thought, angered. Then I began to reason, 'these are the very people who are trying to help me. I had better start co-operating in my own interests.'

I felt bound to volunteer some information: "One of the reasons I left the studio was as a result of the embarrassment I suffer as a result of memory lapses. I remember, in my late teens, I was running the cannery on my parent's farm, and when things got too hot, I just switch off. A person could phone me today, and refer to the conversation we had yesterday, and I would not know what they were talking about. I had to work on it for years to overcome the amnesia. It got better. However, now with the bond being called up, it's re-occurred."

The lists were lengthening. The words, 'insecurity' and 'blackout' were the last two.

The ladies lent a sympathetic ear to me as I continued, "While you're listing spiritual problems, there are another two I can think of: infirmity and osteomyletis. Rob Knight discerned them. The wound on my right leg has been open for nearly twenty years, and my left leg has never fully recovered from paralysis – the ankle is immobile and the toes are clawed.

They all seemed unruffled, and calmly wrote down the two additional words.

After a pause, Ruth asked: "What about rebellion?"

"No! No! I'm not rebellious." I was quick to say. After all, I didn't feel rebellious nor had I ever thought of myself as rebellious.

"What about a familiar spirit?" Ruth continued.

I did not know what a familiar spirit was, but answered, "No." I did not think that I had one of those!

Emily and Frieda were in deep prayer. They discerned a familiar spirit. To my exasperation the intruder's name was added to the list.

Ruth proceeded: "Is there anyone whom you have not forgiven? Because, if there is, that will impede deliverance and healing."

"I've been through the forgiveness conundrum time and time again. I can think of no-one." I cast my mind back over the years of my life right back to childhood. Could there be obscure places in the cameo where an unforgiven person lurked? I saw no-one at first. Then there appeared a tiny silvern light on a slender filament in the pattern – information which I could offer, that may be of help.........

"You must know the scripture about the third and fourth generation – I mean about curses handed down. Well," I continued, noting their affirmation.

"I've got some things against me. On my mother's side, my grandfather was in naturopathy, or so I heard; but I believe there is some history of occult attachment. More recently my mother was initiated into an Eastern cult, and she and my brothers serve a guru in India."

"You're sure in it, girl!" There was love and understanding in Ruth's voice.

The lists were lengthening. Ruth wanted to get on: "Well what else is there?"

There was, of course, something else I knew of, but I did not want to say. I had been nursing the particular secret carefully during the session of ministry, and I continued to remain silent and unrepentant about it. There had been a long mental battle raging since I was born again four and a half years previously: to *smoke or not to smoke*. I remembered the expensive anti-smoke pills; I remembered the hours running into days when I had fought the craving in my body – but it had been no good, and I felt I could not handle that scenario again. I had heard that smoking was rooted in demonic associations, but I reckoned that I would rather hold onto that one for a while!

"Do you believe that God can deliver you? Ruth asked.

I hadn't expected the question. Hesitantly I whispered, "Yes".

The words 'doubt' and 'unbelief' had been added to the list that I could see.

"There is just one thing that worries me," Ruth pried "You said earlier that you told your maid that you were going to visit a doctor this morning."

"Well, I felt sick enough to need a doctor this morning." I never added 'and I have come for healing'.

"Yes, but God wants truth in the inward parts." The ladies noted a "lying spirit".

I was taken aback with indignation!

"Is there anything else in your life that is compulsive?" Frieda asked.

"Well there is something that I have just thought of," I was ashamed to admit, "When I get rattled I can't help using the name of the Lord in vain."

"Blasphemy" was noted.

There were other relics of a past agony that had left their marks: a child who endures the infirmity resulting from an accident such as mine, and endures the psychological pain of having legs maimed below the knee, is wounded in the psyche. These wounds give rise to attitudes, and the attitude invites a demonic presence. Some of these, starting with little brother 'self pity' were listed; and some remained incognito.

Although I was in a miasma, as one who had been sedated before being wheeled into theatre, I knew that the ladies were doing a very thorough job; and I was actually amazed at the professional approach of these people I had known for several years from our Christian fellowship. They had compared notes, and Ruth added to her list any names that were on the others' lists. I heard there were twenty six names! I thought I would die! 'Escape quickly' darted through my mind. I needed to cope with exhaustion to escape the shame. No doubt, I would totter crookedly because of the drugged state I felt, but I was convinced I could still make it to the door and get out! As I was substantiating my decision to do this, the Lord increased the dose of tranquiliser that was keeping me down. However, I was still conscious enough to know full well, that had I not been so sedated, I would not have submitted.

Ruth asked Emily for a straight backed chair, which was placed in the centre of the lounge. Meekly I obeyed when I was told to sit on the chair. The ladies ministering to me were praying, mainly in tongues………

Emily and Frieda stood slightly behind me, but Ruth stood in front of me. She explained the procedure: "We are first going to bind and cast out the spirits of doubt and unbelief, because we can't work on the others until these chaps have gone."

Even in my half-cognizant state I felt a complete fool, but I knew that I must consent to Ruth's plan.

Ruth was firm: "You've got to say, 'you spirit of unbelief, I charge you in the name of the Lord Jesus Christ to get out of me, never to return.' Then you've got to open your mouth and let it out."

I sat in silence. I felt too idiotic to speak. I regretted that I'd ever got into this situation, and severe doubts were cast on the very roots of my faith. 'What would people think if they saw me now?' I thought. I shuddered and went into one of my coughing fits.

"Charmazelle!" Ruth cried, "You've got to command it to go. It won't just come out on its own!"

I grimaced. All embarrassing emotions were subdued by fear, as in the fear of utter helplessness in childbirth – the fear that the baby cannot be born. But the Lord had a word, and in my fear I grasped at it:

"Shall I bring to the time of birth, and not cause delivery?"

Isaiah 66:9

"Oh God," I prayed silently, "Please give delivery!"

Frieda's ministry was one of intercession. She was praying in the Spirit, when God gave her a word. She addressed me: "The Lord shows me you are in chains. Chains!"

Ruth was serene. "Now address the spirit of doubt by name."

"Doubt, get out!" I said valiantly.

"No! That's no good!" Ruth said. "You must address it as a spirit of doubt. And you must tell it to get out in Jesus' Name, because that is the only authority you have got."

I tried again, but remained unconvinced that it would comply, "You spirit of doubt, get out!"

Nothing happened.

"In Jesus' Name!" Ruth added the words that should have finished my sentence.

"In Jesus' Name!" I repeated. Then I started coughing. Emily passed me some tissues, and even ran for a bucket lest I should bring up.

The spirit started manifesting itself to me, for my entire chest cavity felt distended as by a pressure or presence *within*. The pressure went from my chest to my throat and I felt a choking sensation. Then, suddenly, there was no stopping it. I felt a strange type of release as if something had flown from my mouth. Although those ministering to me saw no demon, they *knew* it had left. Frieda was just about dancing because things had started to move. I coughed and coughed to clear my throat and lungs. With joyful voices the ladies all gave praise and thanks to God. They prayed also for the blood of Jesus to cover them, lest the spirit sought re-embodiment.

Ruth went on to bind a spirit of unbelief. I *knew* that I would have to tell it to go, but I reckoned that it would have been so much easier if Ruth could have rebuked it for me. However, there was nothing for it, "You spirit of unbelief," I said, "Get out!"

It would not go. My friends kept praying, and I started praying with them.

Ruth said, "Charmazelle, stop praying. Open your mouth and cough it up!"

I tried. Then I said, "Unbelief........."

"You spirit of," Ruth corrected.

Emily made it uneasy, speaking with authority, "Get out in Jesus' Name!"

Then it manifested itself......... I felt faint. There was a large foreign body in my stomach. "I can feel something here," I indicated with my hand, "In my stomach. Please pray........." I was acting the helpless part again.

Ruth said, "Say after me: 'You spirit of unbelief, I charge you in the Name of our Lord Jesus Christ, to get out of this body. It is no longer your home!'"

I repeated the words after her. All of us were in agreement.

Emily and Frieda laid hands on my shoulders, while I cried, "It's moving up into my chest......... now I feel it in my throat!" Eventually I coughed, and with a loud groaning the foreign body was spewed out with force.

"Oh, praise you Lord," Emily cried.

They bound the spirit and proceeded. Once doubt and unbelief had been dealt with, Ruth simply went to the top of the list. Occasionally they came across one that would not move; they would mark it on the list and move on down to easier game, to return to the more obstinate imposters later.

I was totally amazed at what was going on. It was, in fact, quite incredible that it was happening to *me*. I could just as easily have been in a wide screen cinema house, watching the drama being played out on another actor. As a movie can induce relaxation and sleep, so I relaxed and became sleepy. I would have enjoyed a bed to curl up on and be swept away in a deep and peaceful sleep. I observed that the more evil spirits left me, the quicker the remaining ones went. I realized through the misty realm of semi-consciousness what a labour of love these sisters in the Lord were performing for me. I had the beautiful revelation that this outpouring of love, was a type of anointing of my body with precious ointment. Yes, indeed, that was why the Lord had given me that scripture: *the precious ointment to prepare me for my burial.*

I stood up and found myself embracing these wonderful ladies. I knew that they loved me with an agape love – a love that transcends human affection, and I felt the same love for them.

I wept, "If you did not love me as Jesus loved me, it would not have been possible."

Emily hugged me assuring me of their love. We stood huddled in a foursome; knowing individually and severally that it was the love of Christ for His body, the church that has made this deliverance possible. He had come down from all His heavenly glory to give us of His power, that through Him captives might be loosed!

Ruth had been right through the list, when the Lord gave her a word of knowledge: "Charmazelle, you are holding onto something. What is it?"

I groaned. 'Oh no!' I thought, 'she hasn't found out about the smoking, has she?'

"Come on, out with it!" Ruth demanded.

"Well, I'm dying for a cigarette!" I said, albeit expounding an irrelevant cliché.

"Aha! That's a craving!" Ruth had unearthed another one.

"You have no idea how badly I want a cigarette right now! I don't know how I'll get through another half hour without one. The feeling swamps me!"

"Well, this is the last time you're going to want a cigarette, because we're going to cast out this thing called craving!" Frieda spoke with faith – the evidence of things not seen.

To be quite frank, I would rather have settled the craving with a cigarette than to have it cast out.

Emily took me firmly in hand: "Charmazelle, they've all got to go. The house is going to be swept clean. If there are any left it simply means an open door for the others to come back in. This is very important, particularly as they each come back with seven brothers!"

I capitulated.

The ladies got to work on the demon called 'craving', but I remembered my past futile attempts to give up smoking. I didn't want to go through those withdrawal symptoms again, and go through the mental pre-occupation of where to find and smoke the next cigarette. Then I realized that they were not going to be able to cast the demon out because of my double-mindedness. However, I had to seriously consider what Emily had said about the seven brothers – and that was scary!

Then, amongst the medley of my own thoughts, God gave me discernment: "It's no good trying to cast the craving out. There's another one that's got to go first. It is lodged in the arms, and it is joined, here behind my neck, in a U shape." I indicated with my hands. "It is much more powerful than the craving. It explains why I had such terrible pain in my arms when I tried to kick the habit before."

They laid hands on me and prayed to break the bondage in the back of my neck and shoulders. It did not take long and a tenacious spirit, called 'habit' was sent to dry places.

The way was now opened to cast the craving out. It was centred in my solar plexus, and from there radiated to the pit of my stomach, to my chest cavity, and round to my back. Ruth cursed the thing in a strange tongue, and laid hands on my lower back. Something was identified, as an entity apart from me. My body convulsed, and it was not long before that thing that I was undecided about letting go, burst from me with a cry, and I coughed up a considerable volume of phlegm after it. After that I did not cough again. All signs of the bronchitis I had been down with left completely.

The list had been dealt with, and the smoking had been dealt with; however Ruth, who had had some experience in the deliverance ministry, continued, addressing not me, but any spirits left within me: "This house has been cleaned and washed in the blood of Jesus. Any demons that might remain, come out, I charge you now, in the Name of Jesus!"

Ruth, Emily and Frieda agreed, repeating with one accord, "In Jesus' Name!"

Ruth asked me, "Do you feel anything?"

"No." I didn't want there to be anything else.

They prayed and waited. Ruth received a word of knowledge, "Rebellion."

"No." I answered, thinking, 'would I have given myself up for this encounter if I was rebellious?'

Ruth persevered, "Do you feel rebellious?"

My mind was blank. Slowly I started using stepping stones to think: what was rebellion? I remembered the word from history lessons at school, and the connotation of national uprising came to mind. I had never participated in a protest march; I was never involved in a plot to overthrow heads of state. Therefore I didn't know what Ruth was getting at!

Slowly a different sequence of thoughts started to gel – was it an attitude that brewed within me? I remember that at the age of thirteen, the father of a friend of mine called me obstinate and pigheaded, because I had unbending determination to get my own way. At that age, and given my difficulties trying to walk, I considered my determination a singular virtue: it spelled strength of character. My self will was justified as tenacity, and it was an asset to me in those years; but it was also the antithesis of submission.........

A faint realization began to dawn: it was, maybe, possible that at times, I could be wrong. As my attitude began to soften, the whole truth flooded through, and I got such a shock when I saw it in the spirit, I nearly fell over.

"What is it?" Ruth cried.

"Rebellion." I whispered, shrinking back.

"Have you got rebellion?" one of the others asked.

I groaned: "Have I got rebellion? I've just had a vision of it! It's in my stomach. It goes round and round like a coiled snake – a scaly brown-black rinkhals........."

Emily screamed, "A snake!"

Ruth started praising God. Soon the others joined the crescendo of praise. Jesus was worthy to be praised for He had overcome death and hell and the grave, and to Him was given all authority in heaven and on earth. They were dealing with the symbol of the very devil himself – the snake; but they had no fear, for Jesus has gone before them and defeated that serpent on his own home ground! They were dealing with a conquered foe!

They threatened the snake with the blood of Jesus and commanded it to come out. For some time it would not move, but then eventually that great spiritual serpent broke loose from the hold it had on me, and issued from me, leaving me completely exhausted.

Ruth made every effort to see that I was clean, and that I had been set free from all evil spirits. However, due to my extreme tiredness, several questions she asked received no answers.

She then prayed aloud, *"Heavenly Father, the things that have happened in this house, on this day, will remain as a closed book between the parties here present. Nothing will be spoken of these events, until You permit it. We make this solemn promise to You."*

The Spirit of God made them aware of things that they did not know, for this solemn promise was to be of vital importance to me for a time.........

It was nearly half past three! We had been at it for over four hours! Before leaving we again huddled in a foursome, and they prayed that, for every evil spirit that had left me, a corresponding good spirit would come into me; and that I would be protected by the love, peace and assurance that only the Father can give.

Indeed, the love and dedication of these sisters, and the sacrifice of themselves for me these many hours, was the precious ointment used for the burial of my body. I thanked them. We embraced, and left to go our different ways.

TWELVE

PUT ON YOUR BEAUTIFUL GARMENTS

On the Thursday afternoon when I came home from Emily's place I was like a cat on a hot tin roof. I knew in my heart of hearts that a great deal of good had been done, but I could not come to terms with it. Instead of basking in the joy of the victory, I sank into an irrational attitude of despair. I knew this was contrary to what my reaction *should be,* but it was like post natal depression – after the birth of a baby, the mother is overjoyed to have brought forth life, and relieved that the ordeal of pregnancy and birth is over, but suffers depression. Logic did not help. A feeling of shame and nakedness overcame me. It was a spiritual nakedness – I felt ravaged in my inner being. Parts of me had been exposed that should not have been exposed, and I did not like it. The more I dwelt on the shame of nakedness, the more agitated I became. I paced up and down, challenging the whole deliverance experience. I did not consider the fact that I was no longer coughing - physically healed from a bronchial condition – to be of significance. (How quickly the people built a golden calf, when Moses went up into the mountain to hear from God!) Indecision, confusion and uncertainty assailed me.

When Tim arrived home at sundown, he found me pacing up and down, and he knew that I was distraught. He was shocked and realized that something extra-ordinary must have happened.

In as few words as possible I told him about the deliverance that day, but finished with the plaintive wail: "Now I feel naked and ashamed, and I want to die........."

Tim had listened quietly, but I could see that he had become angry. "Who arranged this meeting at Emily's place?"

"I phoned Emily. I felt terrible this morning. My throat and chest were sore, and I was coughing a lot. First I prayed about it, and I got a scripture from the Lord about burial – 'to prepare me for my burial'. To me that meant I must go ahead and phone her. She *knew* there was more to my request than the healing of bronchitis, so she phoned the others."

"Who else was there with you?" Tim was still angry.

"Ruth, Frieda and Emily. I should feel very good, and thankful to God, and thankful to those who ministered to me, but I don't. I can't explain this feeling of defilement."

"They've done half a job! That is very dangerous. Who was responsible?" He asked in a serious tone.

"All of them – well, no, primarily Ruth, I suppose." Despite the raging fire in my being, I knew that I had to defend them. "They didn't do half a job. They tried very hard to do the whole job!"

Tim was unconvinced. "Unless the house is properly cleaned, they all come back with seven brothers. You were acting like a raging lunatic when I came home. I had better phone Ruth. I don't like what she's done at all!" He moved towards the telephone.

"Love, it's not Ruth's fault." I remonstrated. "She just about moved heaven and earth to do the job properly. I was in a state of total exhaustion most of the time, and they kept finding more demons. I can assure you, they searched to the best of their ability."

The look of anger on Tim's face abated.

"It was no easy matter. It took just about the whole day. Ruth tried very hard. They showed me so much love. That was very important to me."

"I see." He began to understand.

"It's not Ruth's fault that I now have this intolerable shame of nakedness upon me."

Tim paced up and down. I knew he wanted to contact Ruth, but that he did not want to do it in front of me to upset me further. He prayed to God for wisdom, and for the right words to say to comfort me.

However, I could not respond to comforting words. The waters of my soul were troubled, and I myself was amazed at the driving power that kept me going. Something beyond the natural spirited my unrest, and I was drawing on reserves of energy available only from the abnormal secretion of adrenalin in a time of crisis. I walked around the house energetically as though I was in search of something.........

I wanted a cigarette!

'Delivered?' I thought. 'I am supposed to be delivered from smoking! No! I am going to find a cigarette!' I reckoned that it was just plain cruel to go without cigarettes on top of all the other hectic issues.

Tim had been shaken by what he saw in me. He left me for a while and went into the bedroom. He removed a small vial from the drawer beside my bed, and then went on into the kitchen to start thinking about the evening meal.

That gave me the opportunity to slip out of the front door. I had not bought cigarettes that day, because I did not think that I would ever use them again. I went quickly to out neighbour's fence. He was in the garden, using up the last of twilight visibility. I called to him and asked if could lend me a few cigarettes. He was only too willing to oblige.

I lit up immediately, and drew hungrily at the smoke. It had been many hours since I had had access to the precious sedative. The satisfaction was great, because the craving had been great.

After a few cigarettes I calmed down a little. I found an easy chair in the lounge and reclined, wondering what to do next – how to handle the new impasse.

I thought of getting away, even if only for a day. With this in mind I thought of my friend Melanie Hampton. Melanie was a Christian and a qualified nursing sister. She and her husband farmed on the Oribi Flats about forty kilometres inland from our smallholding. It would be a scenic drive through the Oribi Gorge, and I thought that that in itself would do me good. Melanie was also a good conversationalist, and her loving attitude coupled with her professional insight would uplift me.

I stepped towards the telephone, pleased that I had at least one positive thought, after the confusion I had felt since leaving Emily's place.

Melanie answered, "Charmazelle! How wonderful to hear you!"

After the usual, 'how are you's', I ventured to ask, "Can I visit you tomorrow?"

"How lovely it will be to see you! That will be grand!" She said warmly.

Tim was quite pleased that I had made the arrangement, as he knew that Melanie would be good company for me.

*   *   *

When I arrived at the Hampton's farm the following morning, Melanie was very hospitable. On chatting with her, I enjoyed her professional insight. I basked in the comfort of her lounge and we had a non-stop discourse on many things that we had in common. I thoroughly enjoyed sharing with her, and relished the fellowship. We walked around her beautiful garden before lunch, and she showed me beds of flowers which she had successfully cultivated.

After lunch we had no sooner settled down to coffee and a further chat, when we were disturbed by the telephone.

Melanie answered, and then called me, "It's Tim."

Tim's tone was one of loving concern, "I have been talking to Ruth, and we have prayed about you. We both feel that you need further deliverance. Ruth says that there is something that she missed, and she did not have peace when you left yesterday. Come into town and meet me at Frieda's shop later this afternoon."

I flew at him, "Don't be mad! At Frieda's shop – never! People will hear all over town. In any case, I couldn't bear another session. I've had enough deliverance. I don't want any more."

Tim was unable to persuade me further, and we said goodbye, on a very unsatisfactory note.

I returned to the couch where I had been sitting, enjoying the fragrance of Melanie's companionship. She had wrapped me in cotton wool that day, and her ministry had been received by me with heartfelt gratitude.

A little before half past four that day we said fond farewells and I started on the long drive home. As I drove it came to me that there was something in common between Melanie's concern for me and Tim's concern for me. What was it? They were being over protective towards me for some reason.

Did they suspect that I had an escape mechanism that would detonate if things got too hot? I half smiled – that was it......... it had been there for years, safely hidden, but *there*, always offering an alternative. Ruth had missed that one, its name was '*suicide*'.

I drove pensively from Melanie's farm, taking in the details of scenery to left and to right as I went. The Oribi Plain was an extensive flat plateau, boasting succulent young cane that met hazy horizons in every direction. Looking ahead on the road, it seemed it would maintain its perspective endlessly. No one would have thought that shortly the flats would meet the perpendicular walls of a cavernous gorge. Shortly the traffic signs indicated a bend, a drop and a considerably reduced speed limit. The road was cleverly cut into the sheer mountainside, and followed tenuous winds down into the deep chasm. On leaving the cane lands, the vegetation had changed abruptly to sparse bush in sourveld as the road began to drop; and then of a sudden jungle type trees and creepers created a wall of tropical greenery on the right, and plunged to dark emerald depths on the left. The incline of the road levelled to follow a shoulder of land, and widened slightly to accommodate a view site from which one could see from one side of the gorge to another. I did not stop, but drove very slowly taking in the magnificent panorama, etched in rock with abundant green vegetation in bass relief. Looking over the gorge from one high vantage point to another created a feeling of dizziness. Then I started to fantasize: I entertained thoughts of swinging on a wire bridge that was suspended across the gorge. What a masterpiece of engineering it would be to suspend a bridge thus, literally in space, for the river was so far below that the bridge might have been spanned from another star! What a far reaching act of daring it would be to cross over on that bridge; the bridge would sway, and the footing would be insecure, and from there one could slip......... aha!

I shuddered, battling to collect the reins of self control. The wheels of my car were glued to the winding road that had narrowed, and was now descending more steeply. One wrong movement of a foot on the brake or the accelerator and suicide will have achieved its *fait accompli*. I nosed slowly forward taking in the details of the monkey ropes swaying overhead and the trees that canopied over the road at the bends. The steep decline levelled for the hairpin bends, where invariably the clear waters of a little stream would be bridged. The air was warm and clean, but for the mustiness of decomposing leaves. Soon I was at the river, and as I approached the low, narrow bridge I heard the water gurgle as it made its rapid way over countless smooth white rocks. The road out of the gorge was even steeper than the road in. Banks of fern hung vertically on my left; lichen and moss clung to moist rock faces where the road curved inward on the mountain bends. As the road climbed, I suddenly found myself out of the premature darkness caused by cliff faces hung with jungle greenery. Oblique sunlight paved my way; the road changed from gravel to tar; the vegetation changed from untamed bush to cultivated cane. *I had come through the valley*, and I sped forward on the straight, before stopping to turn left onto the highway.

As my car built up speed over the first long, slow hill of the highway, I became acutely aware of time and place: ten minutes to five, the blue-black road disappearing into cane lands ahead, the sides of the cliffs cut away on the rise to even the road's incline. I was hurtling forward into the actual at great speed – but what of the make-believe? What of the wire rope bridge swaying above the deep, deep gorge? And then it happened, in that instant of time, I correlated the actual with the make-believe. I clutched at the frail, spidery filaments of a memory......... What was it precisely? I felt a rhythm and a beat – the cadence of a nostalgic memory. I kept my thoughts very calm and still trying to pick up the pulse of the verse. What was it that brought this dusty file out of the archives of my memory? With the verse came the awareness of a haunting presence, some emissary of the distant past, that I had known in times forgotten. Quietly I waited for my brain to show up the data.........

Yes, slowly it came back. I allowed the beat to repeat its rhythm in my mind; then, as it repeated itself, I remembered – it was a poem.

"All glory to God!" I said aloud, for I knew that the Holy Spirit was bringing to mind something long forgotten. I could not consciously have called up this poem; recollection of the beat was given supernaturally.

I steadied the car down from a hundred and ten to ninety kilometres per hour as the road came over the brink of a hill to reveal a long winding downhill. I let my mind drift on the topic of the poem. I remembered that I had written it when I was thirteen. I could not remember the words, but I remembered the picture that the poem illustrated; it was *a horse and rider*. The horse was a dapple grey stallion, with perfect conformation and extravagant movement, supremely graceful, the epitome of equine excellence. I was the rider. As I felt the rhythm of his trot, I felt the metre of the verse. Yes, that was it......... a poem written by Omar Khayyam – "The moving finger writes........." I made up my own words to fit the tempo of the poem; I knew that my words expressed a longing to cross over from life into death, but I could not remember what they were.........

And then I recognized it: '*death*'!

I knew that I had better work fast. Again I glanced at my wristwatch: it was four minutes to five. In all likelihood Tim would still be at the studio, and I would catch him. I wondered if Frieda would still be at her shop when I reached town. Would I catch her? Now that I knew about the spirit of death, I wanted it to be cast out as quickly and unceremoniously as possible. The highway veered left toward the sugar mill, but I forked right to go into town. I held my car on the speed limit maximum. Hopefully I would still catch Tim and Ruth.

Of course I knew now why I had been so harassed, distressed and unstable the night before. With the many pawns of the front ranks gone, the two remaining imposters had nowhere to hide.

I drove down to our studio, and was relieved to see Tim's car there.

"Hello," he said, as if he knew I was coming, "Ruth and Frieda are expecting us.

Frieda and her daughter Patti ran a clothing boutique in town. "I'll drive my car there. Will you follow?"

Frieda's boutique occupied the first floor of an oldish building. There was a direct flight of stairs from the street to the shop. The large premises were artistically decorated. Stands of mod clothing were boldly displayed throughout the spacious showroom. Handbags, bathing costumes and accessories hung from a wall behind the counter at the entrance. Frieda was lost in a colourful mosaic as she dealt with a last, late customer. As she rang the old fashioned till on the glass counter she smiled at us, and with a nod of her head indicated a place of privacy at the back of the shop.

Ruth met us there and offered us a seat on an old studio couch which was obscured from the entrance by various clothing stands. Patti came to greet us and offered us some tea.

Despite all that I had learnt, and all that had happened, I again started to feel silly, nervous and withdrawn. I recoiled from the thought that this deliverance experience would become a talking point of the small town community. The cold horror of having the episode misunderstood gripped me. When Frieda came to join us and I was voicing my pessimism: "If this story gets around, I'm leaving town! I could not live knowing that people *knew* about the shame and nakedness I felt last night. I would rather end the whole affair called life!"

Ruth was triumphant. She waved aside my pathetic cry with the victorious words:: "Honey, why do think the Lord gave me that prayer yesterday? Because He knew how you would feel today! We are all bound by that oath. Nothing will be revealed until it is time."

I maintained a sullen silence.

Ruth was bursting to impart good news: "Charmazelle," she cried, "Frieda and I have a word for you!"

I was still like a crushed, wounded bird that could not fly. I did not want a scripture!

"We're so excited! It's so wonderful!" Ruth exclaimed as she paged through a bible.

I wanted to retract from the scene: the needle of my emotional barometer had swung negatively from joy and affirmation to despair and hopelessness, and lay as far to the left as the gauge permitted. In the natural it is still easier to keep the old spirits, live with them, and die with them. In the natural no-one wants to admit, I need help: set me free. I regarded Ruth's exclamation with indifference.

"Here, here, I've found it!" Ruth held the open bible, "Isaiah chapter fifty two."

Tim was standing with his arm protectively over my shoulder, and he held me a little closer while Ruth's voice pealed forth as clear as a bell:

> "Awake, awake!
> Put on your strength, O Zion;
> Put on your beautiful garments,
> O, Jerusalem, the holy city!"

Isaiah 52:1

Ruth looked at me lovingly. "You are Jerusalem. You are the holy city! This is God, speaking to you, His believer."

I thought of clothing and of beautiful garments. How precious after the spiritual nakedness I had felt. It was new to me that I was Jerusalem. I softened, and convinced myself I must accept God's word to me at this time.

Ruth continued:

> "For the uncircumcised and the unclean
> Shall no longer come to you....."

Isaiah 52:1 (continued)

"Oh Charmazelle, what a promise!" Ruth cried. "Do you know what that means? That is God's promise to you that the demons we have cast out won't come back."

> "*Shake* yourself from the *dust*, arise......."

Isaiah 52:3 (italics mine)

That was it! Tim and I looked directly at one another. We understood. I had told him about the scripture, and if they do not receive your testimony *shake* off the dust from your *feet*. I quaked with the warm glow one feels when one is aware of the Holy Ghost at work; my attitude changed from indifference to keen interest. Tim was dancing in the spirit.

Ruth repeated the line she had read, then continued:

> "Shake yourself from the dust, arise;
> Sit down, O Jerusalem;
> Loose yourself from the bonds of your neck,
> O captive daughter of Zion!"

Isaiah 52:2

Frieda was boxing the air. She was the person who had seen me in chains.

Ruth went on:

> "For thus says the Lord:
> 'you have sold yourselves for nothing,
> And you shall be redeemed without money.'"

Isaiah 52:3

That was also significantly prophetic to my situation. I had always considered my problem to be a financial one; and here God was saying that I would be redeemed without money.........

> "For thus says the Lord God:
> 'My people went down at first
> Into Egypt to dwell there;
> Then the Assyrian oppressed
>   them without cause.
> Now therefore, what I have here,'
>   says the Lord,
> 'That my people are taken
>   away for nothing?'
> Those who rule over them
> Make them wail,' says the Lord,
> And My name is blasphemed
> Continually every day"

Isaiah 52:4-5

I caught glimpses of pictures from my childhood. My father had come back injured after world war II. He turned to alcohol, as many men home from active service do, to cope with the memories of the trauma. There were painful scenes of blasphemy, screaming, shouting and howling, as my mother could not cope with the liquor.

"'Therefore My people shall know My name;
Therefore in that day,
That I am He who speaks:
Behold, it is I.'"

How beautiful upon the mountains
Are the feet of him who brings good news,
Who proclaims peace,
And brings good news of happiness.
Who brings glad tidings of good things,
Who proclaims salvation,
Who says to Zion, 'Your God reigns!'"

The promise of feet, lovely on the mountains, struck a note that resounded in my spirit.

"Your watchmen shall lift up their voices,
With their voices they shall sing together;
For they shall see eye to eye
When the Lord brings back Zion."

Was I Zion? Was I indeed Jerusalem? Then this was God's unequivocal promise to *restore* me! I marvelled.

"Break forth into joy, sing together,
You waste places of Jerusalem;
For the Lord has comforted His people,
He has redeemed Jerusalem.
The Lord has made bare His holy arm
In the eyes of all the nations;
And all the ends of the earth shall see
The salvation of our God.

Depart! Depart! Go out from there
Touch no unclean thing.
Go out from the midst of her, be clean,
You who bear the vessels of the Lord.
For you shall not go out with haste,
Nor go by flight;
For the Lord will go before you,
And the God of Israel will be your rearguard.........."

Isaiah 52:6-12

Tim danced again in the spirit. With the imminent bankruptcy we were facing, we had had the feeling of being hounded; but, praise God, here was a promise that we would not go in haste, nor as fugitives, but that God would go before us, and also be our rearguard.

"Halleluia!" Tim cried.

The scripture was exceptional! I was acutely aware of the fact that when God speaks, His words meet their aim; the substance of admonition, yet the stirring of a new hope in our hearts. God brings together the pieces of the disorientated jigsaw puzzle that is our life with one move of His hand: suddenly the pieces fit, and the picture that was broken is repainted in delicate, blending tones. The four of us who stood there knew that we were in the presence of God, and the experience was awesome. An expectant silence prevailed......... I knew that the time had come for me to speak. It was difficult to start. My tongue was fixed to my upper jaw. I closed my eyes, and forced the words out one by one.........

"There is......... something......... I have to tell you......... I.........
I......... have a spirit of *death* in me........."

THIRTEEN

THE HORSE AND HIS RIDER

A single light burned in the rear of Ruth's shop, throwing long, weird shadows from the stands of merchandise which dominated the room. With the darkness that had fallen outside, a corresponding lull had fallen in the town. Patti had left to attend to children. Frieda, Ruth, Tim and I were in complete privacy—cut off, and separated from the world around.

Although they were not shocked at my statement about a spirit of death, the people with me were nonetheless cautious, and sought to hear from the Lord; and so, for some time, they remained quiet and prayerful.

After some time Tim said, "I knew you had a spirit of suicide. That is why I hid those sleeping pills."

"Yes. I know I have a spirit of suicide – and I noticed that the sleeping pills were gone."

"Well, we don't want any of those visitors!" Ruth declared positively.

Tim said to Ruth: "Shall I go and get John Elliot? He has some experience in the deliverance ministry." John was a young pastor who lived near the centre of town.

"Forget it!" I yelled, "If there's another man around here the demons won't come out!" I thought of the love that Ruth and Frieda and Emily had expressed toward me, and how important it was to me. It was difficult to be definitive about it; I couldn't explain the whole emotion to Tim just then.

Ruth and Frieda confirmed my wishes with a slight turn of their heads to indicate the negative.

"Okay." Tim knew he had volunteered a bad idea.

Shortly, the people with me started to pray, and we could feel the presence of God manifested by the Holy Spirit around us. We sang praises to God, for we knew that God inhabits the praises of His people. We praised Him for bringing us together in our present circumstances, and thanked Him for the many miracles that had already been performed. At about half past eight that night, the trio ministering to me started to do earnest battle with the giants, 'suicide' and 'death'.

Ruth was asking questions – deep, personal, soul searching questions. She would stop at nothing; she felt that she had to get to the bottom of the situation, and get the victory *that night*. She would not have trusted me out of her sight, now that those two spirits had been revealed.

"What makes you think you have got a spirit of death?" She asked.

"When I was driving here back from Oribi Gorge late this afternoon, I felt the beat of a poem I had written – like remembering the nostalgic beat of a tune heard long ago."

"A poem?" I heard three voices.

"Yes a poem that stirred a longing in my soul. I felt the throbbing strains of the elegy come back to me after long, forgotten years. As a horse's nostrils flare in the wind at the excitement of a gallop, so a longing spurred my heart at the memory of the danger and the excitement. And then the vision of a horse and rider came to mind."

"A horse and rider!" Tim exclaimed, "What did Rob say? *'A horse and his rider is against you!'*"

"Tell me about the poem." Ruth said.

"Well, it was a poem that I wrote when I was thirteen. It portrays me, as I was at that age, riding a very beautiful dapple grey horse. I remember that, when we were children, we had "dream horses" – magnificent creations of our imagination. The horse would be exquisite and its every movement would be a rhapsody of grace. My dream horse represented the epitome of my heart's desire.

"The dapple grey stallion that the poem described was a horse for kings, with arched neck, nostrils flaring red in the wind, a majestic head carriage, and extravagant movement.

"His hooves were symmetrical, round and polished, characteristically poised in the high-stepping movement of Spanish dressage. He was the progeny of a prized royal bloodline, and displayed the pride of his ancestral heritage; with the conformation of a young Warmblood, the grace of a Thoroughbred, and the courage and stamina of an Arab. A flowing silver mane danced in rhythm with each step, as he moved unflinchingly forward at his rider's command. His ears were pricked and the blue-brown watery recesses of his eyes were keenly focused on the way ahead, eager for the journey that we were to travel.

We walked a cobbled road, wet and moonlit. The road became a track and the stones gave way to turf underfoot, and the horse changed gait into an elevated trot, nevertheless steadily covering ground. We left the territory of life to pass on into the territory of death......... and then, I was riding in the clouds. My horse had no fear, and stepped eagerly forward, and I marvelled at his courage! However, I too, had no fear of the way into death. I had left the earth, and I had all that the here-after had to offer me: no more longing, no more pain, no more crying. I had all that I wanted: the horse and the here-after. I felt the regal glory of a queen as I rode – ethereal, an experience beyond what this earth can offer. The romanticism was all the more poignant for the fact that I had all the horse's power at my command – I was no longer limited by the physical disability of my own human, crippled body. We stepped high on the fringes of the clouds; we crossed the line that separates life and death – the known from the unknown. I had hated the known, and therefore I was willing to embrace the unknown. That other world had long beckoned to me with subtle promises of a better realm."

"You were talking about the beat of the poem. What was it? Ruth asked.

"Oh," I said, and closed my eyes as if to better feel the rhythm that had been recorded in the distant past of my memory, "Yes," I said, "The beat was the beat of a poem by Omar Khayyam……… what was it?" I paused, waiting to recall, "Yes: the moving finger writes………" I left off as I could not remember the poem.

"Could you write the poem down?" Ruth asked, and she then looked for a pencil and paper.

I found it easier to remember with pencil and paper in front of me. Initially I could only remember the first line, but as I started writing, the rest came back to me line for line:

> *The passing rider rides,*
> *And, having passed, rides on.*
>
> *The beautiful one underneath her*
> *Is shining and dappled grey.*

Onward their death path they follow,
Onward, oh onward to death!

For I live for the love of dying,
And my horse he knows no fear!

"It's really rather childish, when you look at it now." I said as I passed the paper to Ruth and Frieda.

In one accord they prayed a positive and powerful prayer: "Oh God, we call on your might to overcome......... In the Name of Jesus we cut off the effects of this poem forever in Charmazelle's life." With that they destroyed the paper.

"Now you must command the spirit of death to come out of you!" Ruth said.

After several attempts I felt that it was hopeless. Weariness and weakness overcame me.

The others addressed the demons, telling them that the blood of Jesus was against them, but the two giants were tenacious. They took a breather, and the conversation drifted onto the subject of being slain in the Spirit. I had always marvelled at this demonstration of God's presence and power at work.

To my surprise, Ruth asked, "Would you like to be slain in the Spirit?" as if she were saying, 'would you like a cup of tea?'

"Yes!" I cried.

Ruth placed her hands on my temples, and prayed in other tongues. Within a short while, I rocked on my heels and fell over backwards.

I remember the trio ministering to my spirit when I came round. I was lying quite comfortably on the floor, unaware of what had happened.........

Then I gathered from my ministers, *they left while I was asleep!*

It is wonderful, in fact truly amazing, how the Spirit of God works with the spirit of man when the person is unconscious.........

I stood up, and we held hands, sang and praised and glorified God. Tim opened a bible at Exodus fifteen, and with one loud voice we exalted almighty God:

> *"I will sing unto the Lord*
> *For He has triumphed gloriously:*
> *The horse and his rider*
> *Hath He thrown into the sea."*

Exodus 15:1 Authorised King James

Ruth took the cue from the previous chapter of Exodus, and in her vibrant, enthusiastic manner, ministered about the Egyptians who had been drowned in the Red Sea – likened to the evil spirits that had left me. She added with excitement:

"… and you shall see them no more forever."

Exodus 14:13

"Glory, what a promise!" I cried, worshipping God.

Tim was waiting with another scripture, as if God was showing us that the bible was written that men might be set free:

"And your covenant with death shall be disannulled; and your agreement with hell shall not stand......."

Isaiah 28:18 Authorised KJV

Frieda was boxing the air as she whirled round in a victory dance!

Ruth said "The strong man has been dealt with! Halleliua!"

We stood in a foursome, rejoicing, and hugged one another, before going to our separate homes.

FOURTEEN

THE SACRIFICES OF GOD ARE A BROKEN SPIRIT

Tim and I drove home in separate vehicles. Patti had taken her mother's car to get home earlier and attend to her family, and Tim had offered to drive Ruth and Frieda home after the session of ministry.

The road home led downwards from the town, winding steeply through bush, before levelling out where it followed the banks of the Umzimkulu River. As I drove, alone in the darkness, contemplating the incredible events of the last two days, my flesh screamed for a cigarette! Although I was delivered from the spirit of the habit of smoking the previous day, the flesh had not yet come into line; more-over I had been smoking at Melanie's place that day, whether to cope with my cravings, or in an attitude of nonchalance, I do not know. I was aware of the tall reeds along the river's edge to my right, and the steep hillside, sparsely dotted with sub-economic dwellings on my left, as I travelled the darkened road that led to the sugar mill. Involuntarily, I simply reached across to my handbag with my left hand and deftly extracted a cigarette from the packet. I drew my hand up toward my lips, but before the cigarette touched my lips, a reflex caused me to bring my hand swiftly past my face and fling the cigarette out of the open window on my right. Then I quickly took the packet of cigarettes from my bag, and let them fly into the reeds after the discarded single.

When I arrived home, I was thankful to find the children asleep – my little maid, Tamara had been keeping a silent, but competent vigil in the house. I bade her go with promises of extra pay for the late hours, and then I prepared supper for Tim, as I knew he would want to eat when he got home. I was restless and made a hot drink for myself. The cigarettes which I had borrowed from my neighbour the previous day were in my dressing table draw, and they were beckoning to me – the 'just one' syndrome to appease the flesh was justifying itself in my mind. I paced up and down, unable to make a decision. Eventually I got the cigarette into my hands, and lit up. Shortly there-after Tim arrived home.

I heard him come into the front door, and called, "Hello......... there is hot food on the stove for you."

He fetched the food and walked through to the bedroom with the tray in his hands, which was unusual, as the dining room was right next to the kitchen. He saw me smoking!

"After all that has happened, are you still smoking?"

It was foreign to Tim's nature to enforce his will on anybody, or to instruct another person to do anything. In all our years of marriage, he had certainly not ordered me to do anything. I was aware of this, but there was another factor at play, another new dimension that I still had to enter to......... Here, then was my first rude handling of the many faceted jewel, *obedience*!

I said with pique: "Well, *you* tell me to stop!"

Tim walked over to my side of the bed, took the burning cigarette from the ashtray, stubbed it out, and said: "Stop smoking!"

That was the end of that – I never smoked again.

There was the stirring of a new emotion, a principle unfolding a new dimension that was strangely thrilling......... The *seed of obedience* has to be planted *spiritually*. Deliverance had ploughed the ground for this seed to be planted.

* * *

When the first, faint predawn shafts of light filtered into my bedroom windows next morning, I knew that it was the advent of a new life for me. This new life was heralded by a word from the Lord which had awakened me, bringing me out of sleep into the consciousness of a glad day. The inner witness of the spoken word I received was to be a staff on many future occasions:

> "Although you are healed in the spirit,
> The symptoms linger on in the flesh."

Praise God! That word would enable me to cope with symptoms in the future. (We pray for healing and we are discouraged because we do not receive it. Many times the miracle has been done in the heavenlies, but we do not see the evidence. If we could just keep our faith alive in the natural, we would see the effect of answered prayer in due time. However, we lose the blessing because of doubt and lack of patience.) I had come out of a land of drought into a land flowing with living waters, and I would be able to remain there as a result of this word, although I had not yet seen the *manifestation* of all the miracles I wanted.

To be set free from evil spirits by the Spirit of God is the most cleansing, strengthening, uplifting, renewing experience a person can have. We become equipped for battle such as we never have been before. No foe frightens us. When we have seen into the spirit world, and know the devil's modus operandi, we are no longer scared of the fight. Fear that lurks in ignorance has been dealt with. We know the outcome – our Victor has gone before us; we have donned a garment of spiritual strength, undreamed of in the state of our bondage. The bible says we become citizens of another commonwealth – a commonwealth indeed, where our minds are able to be renewed.

Later that morning, when Tim had left for the studio, and the girls had gone to school, I threw my bedroom curtains open to the spring sunshine.

"Healed in the spirit – glory to God!" I shouted.

Our smallholding was canopied with a sky of azure blue. Over the sugar cane hills the sea could be seen, and ever such a gentle breeze wafted from the waters, from the south-east: a promise of rain.

I reached for a bible to find words of life, topical to the theme on which the Holy Spirit was enlightening me, and I found these words in Deuteronomy, chapter thirty:

> "See, I have set before you today life and good,
> death and evil."

> Deuteronomy 30:15

I was encouraged and jubilant: God gave us a *choice*: life or death. In my mind I visualized a road in bush country which forked to left and to right. We could choose which fork to take: to the left death and adversity, to the right life and prosperity.

I was excited and wanted to learn more about this scripture. What qualifying factor was there to enable us to take the right hand fork? Ah, I found it further down, in verse twenty:

> "By loving the Lord your God, by *obeying* His voice,
> And by holding fast to Him."

Again, that thump! And the newfound emotion pulsating through me......... I don't know if I was a disobedient child, perhaps so, for my parents might have given in to appease my suffering and disability – but, certainly, I never liked the word obedience.

There was chemistry changing in my body.

*   *   *

A heated conversation was in progress one Saturday afternoon at my parent's farm.........

My young sister, Pauline had been frustrated by her thwarted attempts to compete in the recent South African Junior Show Jumping Championships. Pauline had been aware that one circumstance after another was closing in on her riding career. Although Duhallow's condition had picked up since the course of vitamin injections, the fact that she knew he had a terminal disease clouded her future with this horse.

"With the droughts that we have had, and the sugar farming being so tight, I know that I cannot ask Mom and Dad to give me another horse. I feel that I must give up riding. I want to sell Duhallow." Pauline said addressing me.

"It's illegal to sell him and not disclose the nature of the disease." I remonstrated.

"How do you know?" My mother asked.

"It happened to be a topic of conversation that I had with a vet recently." I answered "But, I tell you what." The kernel of an idea was forming in my mind......... "I'll buy him."

My mother was astonished. "You can't afford to buy him. You can't afford to buy any horse at all, let alone a sick one!"

In the natural I knew that I couldn't afford Duhallow, but I knew that God could supply the money for me to buy him – and I knew that God could heal him. "My offer is five hundred rand."

"It's a deal." Pauline said.

"Well!" My mother exclaimed, unable to understand the transaction.

A day or two later, my friend Melanie Hampton, who lived on the other side of the Oribi Gorge phoned. After the usual greetings, she said: "I have a private income – it's not much, but I want to share what I have with you. In fact, the Lord has shown me to minister this income to you, so that I, in turn, can learn to be more dependent on my husband. But there is one condition. The money is for you personally. It is not to be used in your business."

"Praise God!" I cried. I knew that that was God's provision for the purchase of Duhallow.

During the course of the next few days, I rode Duhallow the ten odd kilometres through canelands from my parent's farm to our smallholding, *Sanderstead.* He was installed in a stable alongside Lucy and Jill's ponies.

By this time, I had returned to the studio on a full time basis, as I was more than aware of the fact that Tim needed me, and that I had my own unique ability to generate turnover.

One Monday morning, Tim suggested that I go riding! This idea was contrary to my sense of responsibility, but I thought, 'Well, as Tim has suggested it, and as he is scripturally my head, I should go ahead and do it'. And this was the advent of the substance of a new thought process: '*It is more important to submit to Tim, than to go to work*'.

The chestnut put his ears back when I came to the stable to bridle him; but that did not frighten me, as I had been handling horses almost all my life.

Sometimes a horse with bad stable manners, was a pleasure out on a ride. Soon I had him tacked up. I mounted, and we tracked downhill toward the Umtentwini River, about two or three kilometres away. It was most enjoyable to ride a horse as well schooled as Duhallow! He was responsive to the slightest aid, and his keen step thrilled me.

Shadows were thrown across the riverside track by the bank of dense trees and undergrowth on the upper side. Early morning light came through the bank of greenery in shafts of yellow, lime and olive. Brown-black shadowy patches separated the iridescent shafts. The river water, brown and shallow, moved over a stony bed on the lower side; sometimes in full view, and sometimes blocked from sight by bush in the in the bends of the creeks. Would Duhallow shy at the strange effects? I braced myself, tightening the grip with my knees on the saddle, and held the reins with a little more contact. I had been riding Pauline's stocky old fourteen three hand show jumping pony on outrides with Lucy and Jill; and it was a far cry from the handful I now had beneath me. I had not ridden a horse of this calibre since the heyday of my riding as a teenager. Even in those years, I had never aspired to the standard of riding that Pauline had attained, nor had I had the exposure to competitive show riding. Pauline had her walls lined with rosettes. Unlike me, Pauline had made the grade; and everybody knew it. Lucy, no doubt, would follow a path of similar accolades.

The moist, early morning air was exhilarating in the shade of the trees along the river; and Duhallow brought me through the avenue without shying or spooking at anything. There was the occasional crackle of a breaking twig underfoot, but otherwise his hooves struck the soft road noiselessly. We moved with mercurial ease, combining swiftness and silence; and we moved as one – horse and rider united in flight, at a pace that man alone could not sustain. From a collected canter, the horse's gait increased to a strong canter, as the road veered uphill away from the bush that ribboned along the river bank. As his canter lengthened our strengths and weaknesses merged together in compensating values, and I was aware that I had to be in command, or he would run away with me.

Soon we were into sugar cane lands, and the road straightened to reveal a long, slow hill, flanked by tall cane on either side. When Duhallow saw the cane road, and felt the soft turf underfoot, his cue was to gallop! His ears were forward, his coat gleamed red in the morning sunlight, his mane was effervescent gold, white and russet froth. As I tried to hold him, his neck arched, with head bent at the poll, and he pranced without gaining much ground, in an endeavour to be let out into the gallop he so wanted, and he strained at the bit until I let him go. He plunged forward with impulsion to lead first with the off, and then with the near fore......... The gallop was thrilling, albeit the pace was daring. My eyes watered from the speed, and I felt a rush of adrenalin before we reached the summit of the hill.

After the gallop we moved at a brisk walk from cane lands into forest. The shade overhead was most welcome. The going changed from swollen turf to mulched clay loam – it was magnificent riding country. The road turned homeward as it wound through the forested hillside, and the horse quickened his gait by instinct. My thoughts were far away, and my body was relaxed. I noted a sandy bank about a metre high adjacent to the road ahead. This led to a track through the trees, where I could enjoy a canter. I brought Duhallow from a brisk walk to a collected canter, turned sharply to the left, and gave him the aid to jump the bank. Although he was faced at the bank from an oblique angle, he did not hesitate, but jumped powerfully up the bank to the higher ground beyond. He was sensitive to my command to skirt the odd sapling that was growing out of line. He did this often with a change of leg, and the movement was achieved with utmost grace and balance. I was aware that, had it not been for Pauline's hard work schooling the horse, it would not have been a pleasure to canter the track and dodge its obstacles with speed and precision.

As the track petered out, I brought the horse to a free walk on a loose rein, and made my way further on to a shady road through the gum trees. While I enjoyed the gait of my horse's extended walk, God showed me a picture. The picture was of a chain with four links, each link representing an aspect of the progression of a mindset.

The horse waits in the stable at its rider's pleasure – a type of *sacrifice*. What value is the sacrifice if the horse is unbroken, unschooled or stubborn? To be of value, a horse must be trained to be *obedient*. And what value is reluctant obedience? The delight is to be *willing*. Only then, after sacrifice, obedience and willingness can the horse be of *service*!

The quality of willingness in Duhallow is what made him such a pleasure to ride. I loved his enthusiasm to go forward. A schooled horse is also much more of a pleasure to ride than an unschooled one. To serve as a show horse, and master the courses in graded show jumping and dressage, instant obedience to the rider' aid is needed, coupled with willingness that spearheads the way, and draws on reserves of ability and courage in its wake.

God had now shown me the chain of progression in the submissive qualities of a horse. What of a person? His people have to be a living sacrifice, obedient to His word, willing and eager; and when the first three links of the chain have been welded one into another, then only can the fourth link be added – then only can a person be of service. Shall the price of a horse not be determined by the service it renders to its master? Service also relates to salvation, and, as I rode, I recalled a scripture:

> "'They shall be Mine,' says the Lord of hosts,
> 'On the day that I make them my jewels.*
> And I will spare them
> As a man spares his own son who serves him.'"

Malachi 3:17 *literally: *special treasure*

The dark, soft, moist forest floor led homewards. Duhallow continued briskly on a loose rein. Once I got home, I intended to devour scriptures, starting with the topic of sacrifice.

I remembered the day when I was ill with bronchitis, and the bible had literally fallen open at Romans, chapter twelve:

"Present your bodies a living sacrifice…"

Romans 12:1

I was as much horrified by the very thought 'sacrifice' at the time as my parents would have been. They would have considered it a primitive, barbaric concept. The very subject which my family would have thought to be in bad taste now became the focal point of spiritual teaching that was quickened to me. I cross-referenced thoughts and scriptures, which brought me into a whole new vista of my relationship with God.

There was a sacrifice ordained on Mount Sinai: it is a *continual* burnt offering, a soothing aroma, an offering made by fire unto the Lord. The sacrifice has to be perfect, without blemish, a sweet smelling savour unto the Lord. The libations and offerings made to the Lord in the Old Testament have a counterpart in the New: could I be continually offering myself, a living sacrifice to do His will? Could I be a sweet smelling savour, a soothing aroma to my Lord? Was my life the aroma of sweet smelling incense in His nostrils all the time? For these were the requirements of God………

For me, certainly, there had to be a starting point – a point at which I was *prepared* to offer myself a living sacrifice. I had to make a decision to enter into the fullness of what Jesus had done, by being the perfect sacrifice without blemish. The scripture says in Ephesians, chapter five:

".…. and walk in love, just as Christ also loved you, and gave Himself up for us, an offering and a sacrifice to God as a fragrant aroma."

Ephesians 5:2 NAS

We become, as it were, a gift to the saints, a fragrant aroma, an acceptable sacrifice, well pleasing to God. In the book of II Corinthians, the scripture speaks beautifully and descriptively of this sweet smelling savour:

"For we are a fragrance of Christ to God among those who are being saved and among those who are perishing.

To the one, an aroma from death to death, to the other an aroma from life to life……."

IICorinthians 2:15-16 NAS

Rob and Dalene Knight, the friends who had prayed for Tim and I, and who had nurtured us through the early steps of our Christian walk, had a scripture from Samuel I hanging on the wall of their study. (I don't think we had seen these dear folk since Rob prophesied that I had a horse and his rider against me) I recall that I used to consider the particular scripture obnoxious. How my understanding had changed; for now the words were precious!

"Has the Lord as great delight in
Burnt offerings and sacrifices
As in obeying the voice of the Lord?
Behold, to *obey* is better than sacrifice,
And to heed than the fat of rams.
For rebellion is as the sin of divination….."

I Samuel 15:22-23

From the book of Hebrews I learnt about a *type* of *continual burnt offering*. When Jesus came into the world, He said:

> ".......Sacrifice and offering You did not desire
> But a body Your have prepared for Me
> In burnt offering and sacrifices for sin
> You had no pleasure.
> Then I said, 'Behold, I have come –
> In the volume of the book it is written of Me –
> To do Your will, O God.'"
>
> Hebrews 10:5-7

The concept, 'to do thy will, O God' is the ultimate of sacrifice, obedience, willingness and service, and requires a renewed mind, which was a blessing that followed deliverance. I was excited by a flood of understanding about the scriptures; and I wanted to continue to learn more and more of God's word. In Psalm fifty one I found words of utmost significance on the theme that had been my subject of interest:

> "For You do not desire sacrifice, or else I would give it.
> You do not delight in burnt offering.
> The sacrifices of God are a broken spirit,
> A broken and contrite heart - ...."
>
> Psalm 51:16-17

Halleluia! The realization came to me that one has to go *beyond* sacrifice – sacrifice as in burnt offerings – the sacrifice of oneself has to be spiritually ordained; and this may only happen when the human spirit bows to the divine.

The thought chain formulated that the end of self will is the sacrifice of a broken spirit. The end of a broken spirit is obedience to God. Obedience is made acceptable by willingness; and the end product of willingness is service to the Lord.

FIFTEEN

....PIERCING EVEN TO THE DIVISION OF SOUL AND SPIRIT

Tim and I were invited to a Sunday get-together at the home of Rob and Dalene Knight. Not only did this couple have a royal flair for catering, but the gatherings were exciting because the Spirit of the Lord was present there, and we often met the most interesting people who had come from far and wide to enjoy fellowship. The Spirit would move and there would be miracles. Things happened at the Knight's home that weren't happening in many churches.

How I had changed! In times past I had always been on edge when visiting them, feeling like an outcast or an alien. During our visits I would either sneak out into the garden to smoke, or sneak into the kitchen and wash dishes as a cover while I battled to deal with myself. Now I felt a glorious freedom! I was one of them! There was a flood of peace in my soul – I had equality with the saints. In conversation I could be calm and forthright. I no longer squirmed in the darkness of confusion.

After partaking of an attractively served, satisfying meal, I helped Dalene clear the lunch table. A group of men had gathered in the foyer, and were talking closely. I walked up to them to join Tim. He put his arm protectively around me. Quickly I realized that he had been telling them about my deliverance, and I remained quiet until he had finished his sentence.

Then I remarked almost apologetically, "A legion!"

Rob knew that there was work to do: he disappeared for a while, and then returned with a bottle of olive oil. He sat me in a high backed chair in the lounge, and everyone gathered round me. Most of the people were praising God for the mighty work He had done.

I heard cries of: "Halleluia!"

What Rob had seen in the Spirit was the incomplete healing in my flesh. This was confirmed by the scripture God had shown me, 'the symptoms linger on in the flesh.'

Rob uncorked the bottle, and poured some oil over my head: "I anoint you in the Name of Jesus."

The group was gathered prayerfully around me. The oil ran down from my hair onto my forehead, and down the sides of my face. I wanted to weep! I knew that this oil was for the healing of the trauma resultant from my motor accident, the stress I had suffered with the business over the past few months, and the emotional agony wrought by the demonic powers that had had a hold on me over a prolonged period of time. Here was healing! Halleluia. God's mercy and forgiveness was channelled through the saints ministering to me.

Then Rob prayed in the spirit quoting parts of the word of God from Hebrews chapter four, verse twelve: "Father we thank you that your word is living and active and sharper than a two-edged sword, and we pray for Charmazelle in the Name of Jesus: *that your word will pierce to divide soul from spirit, even as of bones and marrow.*"

That prayer was a most poignant, significant milestone in my healing process. I did not grasp the enormity of the meaning at that time, in fact the words were almost irrelevant, but the Holy Spirit was still to open my eyes of understanding. The group that was praying for me in the foyer dispersed. I wiped the oil from my brow. I felt aglow from the love shown to me by the brethren, and the peace that passes all understanding descended on me.

It was not long before Dalene was at the piano again, and folks were singing and praising God. Rob was dancing and many of the children joined him in the middle of the lounge. Tim, too, would not miss an opportunity to praise God in dance. Rob led the singing to the tune of a gospel chorus that Dalene played on the piano:

> I could have danced for joy,
> At such a wondrous thing;
> Just to know you are the King of Kings,
> The Son of righteousness
> With healing in your wings.
> You are the great I am.

*   *   *

At the time, I did not understand why Rob had prayed over me for the dividing of soul from spirit, which in my natural mind, was not relevant. However, I later found the scripture in Hebrews chapter four verse twelve. In contemplation I realized that there was a separation of soul and spirit that had to take place – not only the leaving of my old self behind and embracing the new creation that I now was, not only the healing of the scarred emotions (and the healing of the scarred flesh which would follow) but a setting apart, enabling me to soar like the eagle into new vistas of understanding. I realized that in the unregenerate man there is a merging of soul and spirit, and very often (as can be ascertained from speaking to most believers) a confusion as to the identity of each. In answer to Rob's prayer, the Holy Spirit performed a type of laser beam surgery in me that would keep me in awareness of the separation at a future time, when I would need to draw on this strength.

The Holy Spirit brought a scripture to mind in the darkness of the early morning one day about mid October:

> "Be ye therefore holy – casting down imaginations and every high thing that exalts itself against the knowledge of your God."

From II Corinthians 10:5

At that time I had been a Christian for four and a half years, and I had heard a lot preached and said about holiness and sanctification. I had always thought it was some state I would aspire to at some point in the distant future, by some means too vague to fathom at the time. There had never been anything finite about holiness as a condition that I could attain to in the prevailing circumstances. I had also heard the scripture from II Corinthians quoted many times, stating that we are not wrestling with flesh and blood, but with principalities and powers and spiritual wickedness in high places. This scripture which tells us to cast down imaginations, ends by telling us to bring every *thought* captive to the *obedience* of Christ.

I had always related this scripture, which speaks of spiritual warfare, to deliverance, but I had never related deliverance to holiness. Here, in the words God spoke to me holiness was linked with deliverance. To become holy, I now understood, was to cast down every high thing (principality and power). For this cause God has given us weapons that are mighty for the pulling down of strongholds.

Just as ideas on sacrifice had repulsed me in my unregenerate state, scriptures on the role of women had caused me to feel uncomfortable, and I used to gloss over them as irrelevant; or perhaps, as something I might take cognizance of at some indefinite time in the distant future.

Now, however, freed from satanic bondage, having seen the precious jewel of obedience, I found that submission was one facet of the gemstone. I wanted to throw as much light from the scriptures as I could onto this facet, and in my search, I found:

"Wives, likewise be submissive to your own husbands…"

I Peter 3:1

Wow! A complete turnabout of my thinking would be needed! The mystery unravelled after reading more on this subject in I Corinthians 11: the woman ought to have a symbol of authority on her head because of the angels.

On one occasion while visiting Rob and Dalene, the topic of a head covering for women came up as a subject of conversation. Dalene had come out of a religion which required the women to wear hats. She explained that this was their concept of a head covering, but actually, what is needed is a spiritual covering; and that, simply, is why women should submit to their husbands. This covering provides the woman with a spiritual status, making a statement to principalities and powers and protecting her from demonic onslaught.

On reading further I found another scripture that I would have to come to terms with, which would have been a stumbling block to my old self:

"Let a woman learn in silence with all submission."

Timothy 1:11

This scripture still tended to stir feelings of discomfort. Then, as I meditated, something started to gel………

In a mathematical equation, if a equals b, then it follows that b will equal a. Therefore if a woman receives instruction with entire submissiveness, it follows that if she is entirely submissive, she will learn.

As I was so eager to learn more of about God and His ordinances, I thought it might be a good thing to try!

I had that inner explosion of joy that comes from revelation knowledge. All my life I had learnt very little about God, and His order for man. I know that I had needed God very much at times, but not knowing God's order, I was unable to receive His promises. I had stumbled on in ignorance, bound by forces I was unaware of. Not for want of crying to God, did I not get the victory in areas that I so badly needed it, such as the healing of the incurable wound on my leg, but for want of being in order! When the principle of obedience came alive in my members, I could come into submission. But I had to seek after and invite it; I had to cultivate submission by an act of my will, and I had to *let it happen*.

I had to steer away from self will, obstinacy, stubbornness, intransigence and rebellion. Then it was amazing how the Holy Spirit encouraged and enlightened me. It was a precious experience of spiritual growth, and a precious time of receiving revelation knowledge.

The romance and emotional enrichment of my marriage was immeasurable......... Men and women are made in three dimensions, body, soul and spirit. The fortification of soul and spirit was not without a counterpart in the body! My body was aroused and tingling, and I desired Tim as never before. After fourteen years the marriage bed had new aspects that I had not known heretofore. There was a calling forth, an exhilaration, an evocation that escapes the world.

And the tragedy is that the world, in its search, tries to find this stimulation in porn, and worse still in child porn; they seek and they cannot find, and the age is sick for want of the Spirit that they do not know.........

*   *   *

Tim and I and our children were privileged to serve the Lord at different times, in different ways.

Peggy Maartens was a new Christian whom Tim and I met at a home bible study group. She was a well groomed, buxom redhead, the mother of two children, not yet in their teens. This lady had been harassed by a husband prone to drunkenness. He was a man who threw his weight around, and Peggy was scared of him at times when his temper was aggravated. He had recently forbidden her to gather with other Christians, or to go to bible study.

Through a set of unlikely circumstances, Tim, our children and I were invited to the Maartens' home by the man of the house himself. At the time of the invitation, Kurt Maartens told Tim that he was prepared to hear about God in his own home, but that he would not go to church, or any organized religious meetings. Kurt was a large man, with dark, wavy hair and an olive complexion. Had he made application for the job of a bouncer at a night club, he would have been taken on immediately. One glance at him, made one realize it would be scary to cross his path! Kurt, however, needed no humble night-club job, as he had his own construction company. In his domain, he had the swollen head of a Nero, and administered his own empire with flamboyant rule.

On the day that we were expected at the Maartens, we Bryants set off – a small contingent of the army of God. However, when we got to their home, Peggy met us with some embarrassment, and explained that Kurt was not there. He had labour working overtime to throw a concrete slab that had to be finished that Sunday.

Tim and I knew that the spirits within Kurt simply could not face an encounter with the truth of the gospel; however, we gracefully accepted Peggy's excuse. Peggy asked us in, and once our respective children had made each other's acquaintanceship and gone out to play, Peggy poured her heart out to us.

"He goes to the pub every night and comes home stone drunk. I wouldn't mind that but he is such a swine that he won't let the children or I sleep. He wakes us all up. He makes me get his supper, and he wakes the children up and scolds them. They are terrified of him. They have to go to school the next day, and they shouldn't be woken out of their sleep to be reprimanded."

Tim and I suppressed exclamations of horror.

"Although he's out every night, he won't let the children and I go out at all. We have to be at home the whole time. I think that's selfish, don't you?"

"Yes, indeed." Tim agreed.

Peggy went on to explain some ugly details of their married life, and pour criticism upon Kurt's character. While I realized that this dear lady who was crying out for help, and had every reason to criticize, I knew that I had to deal firmly with her for her own good. Recent teachings of the Holy Spirit welled up in me:

"Peggy," I said, "I am saying this in love: please stop criticizing Kurt. Kurt does not know that you are criticizing him, but God does."

Tim observed, "God knows what we think as well as what we say."

"Oh!" Peggy exclaimed. She was a keen, young Christian, newly baptized in the Spirit, but at that stage had not reckoned that God knew her thoughts.

"May I tell you a little story?" I asked.

"Yes." Peggy was keen to hear.

"One day Abraham was sitting outside his tent, when three angels came up to him. They said that Sarah would have a son at about the same time the following year. Now Sarah was inside the tent, but she had heard them speaking. She thought that that was funny, and she laughed to herself, 'ha, ha!' You see, she knew that physically she was past her time for childbearing.

A time went by, and then the Lord said to Abraham, 'Why did Sarah laugh?' Abraham then asked his wife why she had laughed. She was afraid so she denied it, saying that she did not laugh. However, God had told Abraham that she did laugh."

Tim was listening quietly, allowing me to minister to Peggy on a woman to woman basis.

Peggy was wide eyed. However I had the impression that she did not know why I was telling her this story.

"What I want to point out is that God knew that Sarah had laughed."

Peggy nodded.

"Okay, that's point number one. Two, then, is that God was able to tell Abraham that Sarah laughed."

Peggy got a fright. "I hope no-one tells Kurt what I say. My life wouldn't be safe."

"God could tell Kurt that you laughed, or that you told us he comes home drunk every night."

"Yes, sure........." Peggy was weighing the implications.

"Point three is that Sarah did not believe God. She believed her own body and mind. She knew that she had stopped menstruating, and therefore could not conceive a child. She limited herself by natural and scientific phenomena."

Peggy grasped a further truth.

"And point four," I continued, "Abraham was responsible to God for Sarah's attitude. He had to give an account for it. That is why the Lord came back to him, and asked, 'Why did your wife laugh?'"

"Food for thought........." That was Tim's voice.

I must confess I was learning as I was teaching. "Yes." I said, and paused to recall a supporting scripture:

> "Obey those who rule over you, and be submissive, for they watch out for your souls, as those who must give account. Let them do this with joy, and not with grief, for that would be unprofitable for you."

> Hebrews 13:17

"That is more than just food for thought," Peggy said, "It is a full course menu for the mind."

"Mmmm." I agreed, "I remember the thoughts I had when the principle of obedience was first quickened to me: 'obedient in what, specifically?' I would ask myself. 'To God's word, yes, sure, but to what else?' I would seek a finite answer, and this was the scripture from which I would get the answer, 'to those who have the rule over you.' However, to continue, we still have a point – number five: when Sarah denied that she had laughed, who did Abraham believe?"

"God." Peggy was pleased that she had the answer.

"God." I confirmed.

Peggy interrupted to pour a round of tea.

After tea, I could see that Peggy wanted to hear more, and I said: "In Genesis eighteen, twelve the same sentence that states Sarah laughed, also refers to her calling Abraham, lord. And, In I Peter, three, six the word says that Sarah obeyed Abraham, and the amplified adds, (following his guidance, and acknowledging his headship over her) by calling him lord (master, leader, authority)........."

Peggy grimaced.

"Are we better than her that we can call our husbands swine?" I asked, and then suffered a moment of regret for the harsh statement. However, I continued, "We don't think like Sarah. We don't follow her example."

"The devil has been around for too long and ruined all the fun!" Tim uttered.

"Amen." Peggy said.

"So we miss out." I ventured.

"So do we!" Tim exclaimed, speaking on behalf of all men!

*   *   *

Of all the scriptures that the Lord gave me during the seven month period that the kernel of this book covers, one of the most pertinent, that ran closest to the bone, was Hebrews chapter twelve. The scripture deals with discipline, and of course, the words of this chapter were all the more poignant to me, for discipline is the tilled ground from which obedience springs forth:

> "My son, do not despise the chastening of the Lord,
> Nor be discouraged when you are rebuked by Him;

For those whom the Lord loves, He chastens,
And scourges every son whom he receives."

Hebrews 12:5-6

The scripture goes on to say that God disciplines us that we may share His holiness, and then come two verses, twelve and thirteen that literally hit me between the eyes:

"Therefore strengthen the hands which hang down, and the feeble knees,
And make straight paths for your feet, so that what is lame may not be dislocated, but rather be healed."

Hebrews 12:12-13

It was exciting to find this correlation between discipline and healing; and hope welled in my heart regarding the unhealed wound of twenty years on my right leg, where a sinus from the tibia had been suppurating all this time. Not for one instant did it ever enter my mind that God disciplined me by giving me the wound! My crutch for some months had been the scripture from Jeremiah thirty, which I was surprised to find documented an *incurable wound*. I had had no idea that the bible made reference to an incurable wound; but my hope was vested in the promise that followed:

"'For I will restore health to you,
And heal you of your wounds,'
Says the Lord."

Jeremiah 30:17

The continual encouragement of the Holy Spirit was precious, and fortified me again and again during this time. When the principle of obedience came alive in my members, (which, no doubt, was only possible after the deliverance) then I could come onto straight paths for my feet so that *the limb which is lame may be healed!*

The words and the facts that led to these revelations were received by faith at that time, but the symptoms of the incurable wound remained until a fullness of time would come. Without deliverance, I doubt that I would have been able to cling to that faith......

SIXTEEN

I WILL PUT MY LAW IN THEIR MINDS, AND WRITE IT ON THEIR HEARTS

The summons arrived in early November! The inevitable follow on of night after day meant that eventually a day would dawn that would bring the devastating news. The bombshell had to explode! The letter of demand that had arrived on my birthday in August had to have its sequel.........

The sheaf of documents was served on us at our home by the Messenger of the Court. The kernel of the formalities set out in the legal papers was that Timothy James Bryant was summoned to appear in the Durban Supreme Court on November the 30th. Until then he was not permitted to dispose of the attached asset – *our property Sanderstead.* By the time the summons was served on us, the addition of legal costs and interest upon interest had ballooned the principal debt to a scary figure.

Once again Tim phoned Rob. "What shall I do?" He asked.

"Nothing." Rob replied, not changing his stance on the advice he gave when the letter of demand had come.

"What about looking for another bond?" Tim asked, no doubt, because he knew that was what I would have wanted.

Tim repeated Rob's reply to me later: "The last thing you want is another bond!"

What could I say or do? Scream and shout and perform, and search the directory of financial institutions for another bond, or submit to Tim, who was submitting to Rob, as unto the Lord?

Some time later Tim said to me: "I am excited to see what God will do in this matter – how He will perform the miracle........."

Despite all that the Holy Spirit had been teaching me about order, I found it very difficult to submit to Tim in the matter of Rob's counsel about our property, but I resolved to do so, and made a courageous attempt at self control.

Throughout the trying period of waiting for the 30th of November, Tim's faith was unflinching; he thought that God would raise up a man who would assist him to pay the debt that he could not pay. A scripture from Colossians became life to him during the tough days awaiting the court case:

> "And when you were dead in your transgressions and the uncircumcision of your flesh, He made you alive together with Him, having forgiven us all our transgressions, *having cancelled out the certificate of debt* consisting of decrees against us and which was hostile to us; and he has taken it out of the way, having nailed it to the cross."
>
> Colossians 2:13-14 NAS (italics mine)

Tim read and reread the *logos* of the quoted scripture trusting, hoping, believing it would become *rhema* – God's specific word to a specific believer in a specific situation. Despite all his fervent prayer it was not applicable to the situation in the way Tim hoped and expected, and this mystery could only be understood years later.

I admired Tim for the way he clung to those words; but I had to take stock of the fact that I did not wholly share in that statement of faith. This caused me tension and strife that I need not have suffered – but suffer I did – because I still tended to look back in case I could make a last, valiant attempt to find a natural way out. I was not yet able to rest in the covenant of God's provision that was being confirmed in my life.

*   *   *

However the Lord ministered wonderfully to us in small, practical ways, during this time of real financial need. On a particular day during that tension-filled month of November, Tim had an appointment with a certain lawyer from whom he had borrowed several hundred rand some months previously to tide the photographic business over. The due date for the repayment of this debt had lapsed on two previous occasions, and Tim knew that this was the final extension of time that would be granted.

"How are you going to handle it?" I asked.

"I don't know, but when I open my mouth to speak, the Lord will give me words."

As always, I could hope, but once again my trust in God did not equal Tim's.

The lawyer's appointment was for ten o'clock that morning. A few minutes before ten a Christian lady, who had actually come to the knowledge of salvation under Tim's ministry, popped in to the studio to enquire how things were going.

Tim talked politely for a while, and listened politely while she testified of recent blessings she had received. Then he looked at his watch. "You must excuse me, but it is five minutes to ten, and I am supposed to see a lawyer at ten."

"Oh dear! You rush off. Don't worry about me!" She said apologetically.

"I'm simply trusting God to put the words into my mouth, because I don't know what to say........." Tim was moving toward the door.

"Why? What is the matter?"

"Six months ago I borrowed six hundred rand. It is supposed to be paid back today."

"Here........." She reached into her hand bag for a parcel, "Perhaps this would help?"

Tim shouted, "Praise the Lord!"

The parcel contained over eight ounces of gold in the form of a beautiful, intricate necklace.

"Now I know why I brought the necklace in to be valued today; and why the Lord sent me here." The lady said.

"Indeed!" Tim cried. He was overwhelmed by the goodness of God. "Praise the Lord!"

There were other such incidents: in particular, the day that God sent a man, whom I presumed to be an angel, up the stairs to the studio. He handed me an envelope, then quickly vanished before I could speak. The envelope contained enough money for a week's groceries!

Tim and I crossed over into a precious period of time during which we were totally dependent on God's provision, received from His ministering angels and from the Body of Christ.

* * *

A few days before the court case, I visited my parents on their farm.

My Father said: "I only wish we could help you financially."

"Yes......... thanks." My answer was fragmented in a sigh; my emotions were a torrent that I could not voice.

My Mother spoke as one well versed in business matters: "What are you doing about getting another bond?"

Now it was spiritual warfare!

She had never had any rapport with Tim all the years of our marriage. She would like me to have told her that I married the wrong man; and she would have agreed with me wholeheartedly – and she would have poured out the heartfelt sympathies she was bursting with! I had to deal with this undertone combined with their approach which was conditioned by natural thinking. I didn't need this. I didn't need to be broken down further by them.........

Could I answer her question by saying, 'Nothing'? I knew very well that I could not. I would have buckled under an avalanche of reprimand and rebuke. I had to put some icing and cherries on the cake.

"Tim is doing something." I justified the lie with the truth that nothing is something. "Please don't worry!" I wailed with a note of finality, hoping to get off the subject.

"But *what* is Tim doing?"

How could I answer the businessman and businesswoman in them? I offered fragmented facts. "We couldn't afford to pay the instalments on another bond, because our business has been hit so hard by inflation, recession, consumer resistance against luxury items, and……… Therefore another bond won't help." Dare I mention Rob's comment, 'another bond is the last thing you want'?

"You must surely be able to negotiate something to prevent a forced sale" My father said.

They would have been horrified if I told them that I was purposely not negotiating anything because of *submission*; because the Lord had told me to be transformed by the renewing of my mind. Even less dared I mention a scripture that said that if you leave *farms* for His sake you would receive many times as much, plus inherit eternal life. No, it would simply add to their condemnation. As it was they believed Tim was a nutcase.

"We have put the place into the hands of just about every estate agent in town!" And I knew as I said it, that it was a hopeless move.

"Have you advertised?" My Mother cried.

"Yes, we've advertised." Tears were in my eyes. "I have no idea how we will pay the accounts for the adverts that brought no replies."

"I think you must advertise again." My Father said, trying to sound hopeful.

"You don't understand……… It's just a waste of time." In a moment of time I had just realized that there actually was *nothing* we could do except wait for the miracle that Tim expected.

"The trouble with you is your religion!" My Mother cried. "You were never poor like this before you started on your religion!"

"What has my religion to do with the devaluation of the rand against international currency? All our raw materials are imported. What has my religion to do with the recession in the sugar industry? We are selling a luxury item people can no longer afford. Where are the sugar barons now? Not long ago we had to vacate well situated premises with lots of walk-in trade for a first floor studio on a quieter street. People don't even *want* to find us anymore!"

"Your religion is nothing but a lot of emotionalism, and your religion has ruined your business, and you know it! And that's also why Tim is doing nothing about your property."

"I must agree with your Mother there!" My Father added.

"Well!" I exclaimed. I was shocked and amazed. I flinched. So the spirits knew! The principalities and powers knew that Tim was doing nothing. I was browbeaten and defeated, and utterly at a loss to defend myself on this count. The incredible thing was that my Christian friends far and wide could not help noticing the change in me. My face had changed. The lines of stress were gone. The change in me was actually a talking point in church circles. They saw me as a new creature in Christ since my deliverance, and confirmed the wonderful work that God had done in my life......... But my parents, those who nurtured me as a I grew up, those with whom I smoked cigarettes for nineteen years, those who should have known me most intimately, those who should have been most grateful, and most sensitive to this change for the better, *did not see it.* To them I was still the same poor, crushed Charmazelle Bryant as ever.

"Did you know that property sales have fallen to an all time low in this recession? I have even heard that lawyers cannot keep their conveyancing departments going."

"Yes, but the wheel always turns." My Father observed.

"The wheel turns, and the horse gallops........." I said.

"What horse?"

"The black horse."

"Black horse?"

"The black horse that is sweeping down through Africa, smiting the people with blindness; the black horse that is the spirit of black power, which gallops on a collision course seeking freedom and liberty. The people are bewitched by vain promises, grasping at an ideal they can never realise, clutching at straws they can never catch."

"That's utterly too poetic and irrelevant. Why don't you talk some sense?" My Mother commented.

"The sense is that the black horse will be followed by the pale horse which symbolizes poverty and hunger. How many small businesses have gone under recently – like our photographic studio? The pale horse will come. It is a sign of the times."

"It is more likely just co-incidence. What makes you think it is a sign of the times? How do you know these things?"

"God's law........" I started.

"What do you know about God's law?"

"God has made a covenant with me........"

"Oh, come on!" They jeered.

I backed off, myself doubting what I was trying to convey. I was at a loss as to how I should cope with the stubbornness of unbelief. The doubt would again assail me: *perhaps they are right and I am wrong.* Involuntarily I ran my tongue over the bridge across my teeth. Was I not bearing the sign of the covenant of God's provision in my mouth, where it was inseparable from me? Why was I fainting with fear when I had the writing of God in my flesh? A scripture came to mind and the words flowed from my tongue:

"God says: 'I will put My law in their minds and write it on their hearts."

Jeremiah 31:33

"How can you believe that?"

"It is a mystery given to the house of Israel."

"You are not a Jew!"

They would not understand if I had said that I was grafted in.; nor would they believe the sign of the covenant, or the signs of the times.

This added to my pain, for the believer's strong emotion is that we want our loved ones to *know and understand* that they might inherit eternal life.

SEVENTEEN

IN THE WORLD YOU WILL HAVE TRIBULATION; BUT BE OF GOOD CHEER, I HAVE OVERCOME THE WORLD

One particular day that warm and humid November, Tim and I sat in the workroom at the back of the studio. The shop was very quiet that day. We were pleased to have the opportunity and the privacy to talk.

The room was well lit from a large, sunny window, as was required for the fine work of retouching, mounting and finishing. Cameras stood on different tripods; flash equipment occupied a large section of a workbench. Artwork and photographs in various stages of completion were propped up on the desk alongside the flash equipment. Photographs, large and small depicting subjects as diversified as babies and sugar mill machinery lay flat or were propped up at various points in the production line. Tim sat on a chair near the centre of the room – encircled by monuments of his art.

Rob had once said to him: "Brother I think that you have some unfulfilled ambition in you."

The surrounding evidence verified this statement. Tim had loved his cameras, his equipment, his photographic works of art big and small; the memory of the acclaim he had received for his work in a small community rang a nostalgic note. He had created a niche market of which he was proud.

I took a seat on a high stool at the workbench and sipped a cup of tea. Tim was sitting at a lower level than I between me and the open window. Back lighting from the window played on his hair – forming an irregular, sparkling halo. His features were bold and handsome in the backlighting, and strength of character showed in his square jaw. His skin was smooth and unwrinkled, and his eyes were very, very blue. I noticed something out of the ordinary – there was a certain ethereal look in his eye, as though he were in this world but not of it. As I became aware of this faraway look in his eye, I observed that his face had changed, not so much in his features, but in his countenance, where I observed a unique, shining quality. His presence revealed peace and joy, such as this world cannot give; for his eyes were on a different horizon, his desires were of a another sphere As I looked at him I repented of the times I had wanted to leave him, albeit the times were passing glimpses of thought. I was overawed as I looked into his eyes.

There was actually no place for words. His expression said it all; and by my recognition of that look in his eyes, I had all the answers to the questions I was going to ask. I thought again of the scripture in Matthew, that I had tried so hard to believe *without doubting* during the days leading up to the court case.

> "And everyone who has left houses brothers or sisters or father or mother or wife, or children, or *lands* for My name's sake, shall receive a hundredfold, and inherit eternal life.
>
> Mathew 19:29 (italics mine)

The memory of this scripture exploded in my thoughts, and led me to realize that Tim had already arrived, while I was still laboriously carrying the load of worry: 'What if we lose everything? What will we eat? What will we drink? Where will we stay?' How could I be so negative as to buckle under the burden of the loss of my earthly possession while my husband was happily adrift on some other lofty plain? More-over Tim was enjoying the victory of having arrived where he had; he had chosen this above the norm of solvency and security that we had been brought up to lean on.

One loud exclamation from me summed up his frame of mind, *"You want to lose everything!"*

"Yes." He said forthrightly, and is face radiated peace and joy.

After several seconds of mathematical deliberation I said, "I see........." and then remained silent, for the equation had been solved; there were no further calculations necessary, no further theorems to apply.

I thought of a moving piece of writing that had been penned by some philosopher down through the ages to the effect that: you cannot easily depart from the place of your labour and strife. It is a place to which you become deeply attached; a place where binding roots have been sent down with trial and hardship; a place that is dear to you and cherished by you for the very reason of this hardship; a place that cannot be left without heartfelt regret and bitter tears, lest the hardship of its acquisition be in vain.

In that moment of time that I grasped and accepted Tim's reasoning. I lost my place of work – my means of income; and I lost the rewards of my labour spent on the home I had built, and the land I had developed. All my desperate striving to hold on to the property had been in vain; all the tears I had cried had been cried in vain. My hope for a buyer at the eleventh hour was hope in vain – for Tim had relinquished his hold!

All the earthly things that we had worked for in our marriage of fourteen years had become as a vapour of dust. Our assets, which had been represented by bold figures on the credit side of our balance sheet for years and years, were simply obliterated by an untimely wind of change......... for Tim had realized other values – values I had not known nor understood; treasures in heaven I had not dreamed of possessing. His treasure was of a different commonwealth. He was no longer fighting for the earthly – he had glimpsed the heavenly.........

All at once I saw another picture, and I got insight into the changes wrought in my husband: it stemmed from our second water baptism – the time Rob baptized us in the stormy sea. From that time Tim was renewed in the spirit of his mind. He was imbued with fortitude and courage, and empowered with new, supernatural zest. His life had been enriched with more than it could ever have been by earthly treasures. Some event had occurred in the heavenlies that had a parallel on earth. This was a mystery. The principalities and powers that were witness to this event now stood at bay. The mystery is the burial with Jesus, for once we have died with him, we rise in newness of life with him; and the powers of the air lose their hold. This unique mystery is veiled in many scriptures, but preached from few pulpits.

* * *

Tim rose early on the morning of the 30th November. He was singing praises to God. I was half afraid to look into his face, lest in my very look I cast doubt upon, and contaminate his faith. I admired his complete trust in God, but I knew that I didn't quite have what he had. As he left for Durban, I reckoned that there were many people who would have thought him foolish to believe that the angel of the Lord would appear in the courthouse......... Tim was trusting God, regardless of what was to transpire in the insolvency court.

When he came home later that day I called anxiously, "What happened?"

"The case was called at about twelve. The whole thing was then dealt with, with the most incredible speed and efficiency. The prosecutor said his piece, reading the charges made by the bank........."

"And then?" I gasped.

"The judge asked me momentarily if I had any defence. Hardly had the word, 'no' come from my lips, when he raised his mallet – and let it fall. That was that."

"In a moment of time......... gone......... The place we loved; the place our children were born into......... *Sanderstead*......... lost!"

"Yes, if you can call it lost."

I looked about me. "The trees we have planted now standing taller than a man; the house we have built; the Spanish arches, and new wing with many finishing touches still crying to be done. Gone – in just one fall of the hammer!"

"Yes." Tim said, "But there is a scripture about mansions waiting for us in heaven."

I could see the tears in his eyes. We embraced.

"Yes." I said, trying to form a picture in my mind of the mansions in heaven.

Tim had a sheaf of documents in his hand. He placed them on a table and we read through the part that said he could be imprisoned without the option of a fine if he disposed of the asset that had been attached without the consent of the Supreme Court. The date set for the sale in execution was the 24th of February of the following year.

The 24th of February......... That was six months after the 24th of August, my birthday, the day on which we had received the letter of demand from the bank calling up our bond.

I walked around the house, restless. Tim stretched out a hand and took mine. I knew that his sympathies were extended toward me in the utmost.

He ran his other hand over the rounded stones of the central fire place that separated the lounge from the kitchen. We found our way into lounge chairs.

"Do you remember when I said, 'let's build an arch over the fireplace'?" He reminisced.

"Yes. I remember asking you, 'how do you build an arch?' and you said, 'it's very simple. People have been building arches since biblical times.'"

Tim acknowledged the memory with a smile.

"I thought, what an answer to give me, and you make it sound so logical! Perhaps it is logical: you just cantilever stones from each side until they meet over the arch."

"You were right. That's how you did it."

I recalled Tim and I collecting the elliptical stones where they had been heaped in the cane roads, so as not to damage the farming implements that worked the ground.

"I wonder how the stones became smooth and round, after all we're three kilometres from the sea?."

That sea view! I wanted to cry. "The oval stones were difficult to set in mortar. How many times they tumbled down, and I lifted them up again, and they became dirty – all covered in slushy cement mix."

"The fireplace worked well."

"I was excited about building an arch, because it would be in the theme of arches that I wanted to build all along the verandah. Now we have those arches........"

"Yes," Tim said. "Yes." He said again, pensive now. "It is hard to part with our creation – the work of our hands."

He took my hand, "Thank God we have each other."

*   *   *

Eventually the abominable summer heat of the Natal February was upon us.

During the earlier part of the month, my father fell and broke his leg. A small piece of the femur or upper thigh bone had been chipped, and he underwent an operation to insert a prosthesis to replace the broken piece of bone. However, infection set in, causing him acute pain, and he was transferred to a Durban hospital for the removal of the foreign body, and the insertion of a pin through the tibia from which the leg could be put in traction until the femur had healed. My mother was not a person who could handle medical emergencies, and she would also not have coped with the hundred and thirty kilometre drive to Durban; therefore it was to me that she looked in this time of trial.

As it happened my father was operated on the day before the sale of our property. I had exhausted my natural hopes and tired my brain out with human plans to save the place. I resolved that all that was left was to leave the matter of the sale to Tim, and escape, as it were, to family commitment, and go and do what I could for my father. I knew what it was to be in hospital, in pain, unable to walk, nauseous after an anaesthetic, and have no-one by one's bedside who cares. Thus it was, that early on the morning of the 24th February, I turned the bonnet of my car toward Durban, and set out on the highway – leaving the matter of the sale to Tim, and to God.........

I arranged to stay with Tyrone and Gaye Summers, who lived in a Durban suburb. They were the folk who had brought their daughter to be photographed with my children's ponies nearly seven months ago. At that time Gaye had prayed that God would bring some-one across my path who could minister deliverance to me. I had packed a bag for a few days, as my mother was convinced that my father would need attention for some time during the early days after his operation.

Durban represented something of a hiding place to me while the holocaust swept past.........

I looked at my watch. I was travelling due north at ten o'clock. What could I feel or think? The judge's mallet had fallen......... would the auctioneer's mallet fall likewise?

Continuing at a steady speed until I reached the big city, I handled the road and the traffic subconsciously. I was like some-one in a dream, as I wound through the maze of city streets, robots and pedestrians to reach the helicopter landing site in front of the hospital on the Marine Parade. Without recollection of parking the car, I found myself being borne aloft in the hospital elevator. The progress of the elevator was sickeningly slow.

When I reached the correct floor – a few stories up – a nurse pointed out the door to the ward. I was unspeakably anxious when I put my head round the door. Then I saw my father, and he recognized me immediately!

"Hello, Charmazelle!"

"Dad, how are you?" I asked with heartfelt concern.

"At last I am out of pain." There was relief in his voice.

"So, the operation was not as bad as we feared it would be?" I asked with trepidation.

"No. It is just such a relief to be out of the terrible pain I suffered!"

"You look so much better than I expected you would."

"I am much more comfortable than I was before." There was a look of peace in his eyes.

My father was in a private ward, and we talked on, unruffled by the hospital routine. He slept intermittently, obviously still under the effects of sedation. Most of the time I simply sat by his bedside, and occasionally I would get up to attend to his needs. Eventually the hospital lunch trolley was wheeled to the door of the ward, and he was served a selected diet. After he had eaten, he again fell asleep, and then awoke suddenly, as from a dream.........

The unexpected question burst from his lips, "On what date is the sale of your property?"

Could I speak? My throat choked on the word, "to.........day".

"Today?" He was surprised.

"Yes. It was this morning." I answered in a voice tempered by anxiety.

He quickly asked, "Well! What happened?"

"I don't know." I kept my tone level with much effort.

"Well, girl, phone Tim and find out! Come on! I'd like to know." He sounded encouraging.

I thought that perhaps he thought there had been a miracle. Perhaps there had been one! I veritably raced down the hospital corridor to the lift, and pressed the button to go down. Impatience gnawed at my solar plexus. However, little did I know what a period of waiting I had yet to endure.

After the slow descent to the ground floor, I made my way through endless corridors, in search of a public telephone booth. Eventually I located such a facility, situated in a type of subway which served as the casualty entrance for ambulances. Such was the architecture of a large, old government hospital. Once I was in the foul smelling booth, I gingerly held the greasy black receiver to my ear, making as little bodily contact with the thing as possible, and I started to do battle with trunk call dialling codes. The year was nine-teen seventy eight. Durban was a hundred and thirty kilometres from Port Shepstone, but a trunk call was required to bridge the gap; and the trunk call procedure in South Africa was slow, exasperating and inefficient in those years.

No matter what number I dialled, engaged signals of varying pitch and intensity bleeped from the receiver. It was, I decided, impossible to reach anyone! I looked at my watch: five minutes past two. I left the telephone booth and paced up and down various concrete corridors radiating from the casualty entrance.

Eventually I returned to the foul confines of the telephone booth. By adding perseverance to perseverance, the trunk call dialling tone finally came through

And my heart leapt as I followed it's prompt by dialling the number of the studio.

The time was half past three, and I heard Tim's voice!

"What happened?" I was almost too scared to ask.

"My biggest problem has been how to tell you." He said.

It was at that point that all hope of a miracle was dashed. My mind started to reel and I felt off balance.......... But wait, perhaps, perhaps Tim was holding back some good news. For what reason does hope spring eternal in the human breast?

"How much?" I cried

"Thirteen thousand........." I never heard him voice the amount of the hundreds, tens and units.

"What?" The frenzied sound sprang from my lips.

We had hoped for thirty thousand, which was a fair price for *Sanderstead*, and that was the minimum we would have needed to pay the mortgage bond and put our photographic business straight.

Tim's voice lost the level intonation. "I have cried before God."

"Did you say *thirteen* thousand?" I asked, knowing that if he repeated it an infinite number of times, I still would not believe it.

Without receiving confirmation, I continued, "What a terrible insult!"

My face became contorted as that of a child about to cry; and tears came without reserve. My mouth was dry. No calculations were needed to figure out that we were ruined. Our mortgage bond and creditors were ten thousand more than the sale figure. There was no horizon in our future, only the blackness of a void. Unlike the vile, claustrophobic situation of the telephone booth, from which I could escape, I was now faced with a situation from which I could not escape. I would never, ever have thought that our little farm could have been sold for such a pittance!

The wretched telephone went beep, beep, and I fumbled to find a coin, which I identified with tear-blinded eyes. There was a click, and I heard Tim.

"Are you there?" He asked.

"Yeah." The sound erupted from my wounded spirit. "What a dreadful insult." I re-iterated. "The bricks I laid, the house we built together, all our hopes and dreams, our children's home – gone for thirteen thousand. I feel sick."

The nauseating smell of urine and tobacco was in my nostrils. That's what you find in the gutter. The prevailing atmosphere matched the crushing news.

Tim's voice came over the line, only to distress me further with the details of the embarrassment. "There were crowds there. Like vultures. It seemed that the whole town had turned out for a morning's entertainment. I was so sure the Lord would have sent some-one to bid among all those people. There was a man in a suit standing round. I thought that he was the one that had been sent, but he never came forward to bid."

I wailed.

"The bidding was so slow. They couldn't get anyone to open the bidding for the amount of the judgement debt. Eventually they opened at five thousand. It went up very slowly. The bank sent a representative to bid. He got cold feet at twelve-five.

I cringed. It was worse than a nightmare. Not only the financial loss, but the shame of having our property kicked around like a football on the courthouse steps, left Tim and I in a state of very low esteem.

"Are you there?" Tim asked again.

I sighed to confirm that I was. The oppressive stench of the tiny phone booth was getting too much for me. Ugly news in ugly surroundings. And what now? Where to? The embarrassment of the forced sale in our small home town further depressed me. Would we be banished without its walls? Who would care for us in our need and in our hunger? Nobody had wanted our property at a fair and reasonable market price. O bitter day! Any word I wanted to speak was caught in a web of silence, swamped in the blackness of despair.

"Are you there?" Tim asked again.

"Yes........." A tiny sound emanated from the drought of my thoughts.

"I know how you must feel. I was ready to renounce my faith, and all I believed in. My biggest problem was how to tell you. I did not want to hear the sound of your crying."

A scripture flashed through my mind about a time when there would be no more tears and mo more crying. Quickly I dispensed with the thought. I couldn't handle consolation. I couldn't speak.

Tim broke another long silence. "Are you there?"

I realized that he, too, must have suffered. "I'm here." I said. "Are you alright?"

"I'm alright now." He said. "Three or four brothers came round to the shop after the sale, and oh, they prayed a mighty prayer. Melanie's husband, Dave Hampton, came out in prophecy. He spoke with the conviction that I have seldom heard on the lips of a man: 'Thus saith the Lord, do you think that *I, the Lord God, will let a son of mine beg?'* God has something in store for us.

But, in the black void that I had entered, the storehouse of rational thinking had been completely ransacked. Where was the next meal for the children coming from?

As I reached the base aspect of hopelessness, the rock bottom of the psyche, there came a turn; a primeval instinct to survive that gave birth to new courage. Likened to the basic animal instinct that the lioness would have when she stalks her prey in the early morning, advancing on soft, silent, sure-footed pads, knowing she must succeed: for there are cubs to feed back at the lair. I stepped forward guided by some latent nerve impulse that took over from my incapacity. A strong, protective, maternal instinct drove me to accept that I had to fight for, nurture, and protect my young. All of a sudden I knew the fighting courage of the lioness.

Tim and the children need you! Fly to their side!

This realization completely cancelled out any previous desire to escape Tim's blundering. For now I only wanted to rush to his side to stand squarely with him.

"I'm coming home!" I cried. "My Dad is much better than I thought he would be. *I'm coming home. I know that you and the children need me!*"

Once Tim and I had said goodbye, I walked from the telephone booth down the long hospital corridor that would lead me to the lifts, and into further corridors to find my Father's ward. *How was I going to deal with the shame of telling him?*

Actually, he was wonderful! I found his conversation to be caring and supportive; where-as for years I had steeled myself against my parent's criticism of all that Tim and I did.

"I am on the road to recovery and I will manage without you until Mom is strong enough to come through to Durban. I see that you are very tired. Please stay the night in Durban. It would not be wise to drive in the dark."

We said our good-byes, and I made my way slowly through the peak hour traffic to the suburb where the Summers lived.

Tyrone and Gaye understood, despite the very few words that I spoke.

"I remember your prayer for me last year when you visited us. I could never have gone through this trial with the impostors, *insomnia, suicide and death* lodging in me. Something would have snapped. I know it. I was too unstable to bear the ordeal."

"Don't give me any credit," Gaye said, "I was purely prompted by the Holy Spirit when I prayed that prayer."

I was still uncertain about whether or not to drive home that night. I phoned Tim, and when we talked, it made me realize how tired I was as a result of the emotional strain. I simply did not have the energy for the drive, and we agreed that I would return in the morning.

I remember lying in bed that night. Questions were flying from my mind like bullets from an automatic rifle. "What now? What next? Where to? Why us?"....... Eventually I slept.

As I awoke in the Summers' home the next morning, I immediately became aware of a most incredible miracle that had happened: it was laser beam surgery. My brain was still agonizing under the gunfire of the many questions, but simultaneously, my spirit was rejoicing, and I heard a melody, strains of heavenly music, bringing a message of hope and promise such as I shall never forget:

> *"In the world you will have tribulation, but be of good cheer.*
> *I have overcome the world."*

> John 16:33 (italics mine)

Now indeed I experienced the separation of soul and spirit, as of bone and marrow, by the word of God which was sharper than a two-edged sword. Rob had prayed that I would receive the separation of soul from spirit; and God had watched over His word to perform it.

EIGHTEEN

THE CROSSING OF THE RIVER

There were practical steps that had to be taken. Fast action was needed to pack and leave *Sanderstead* within four days. Tim and I wanted to be gone from there by the first of March, 1978.

When Ruth had said that she had a scripture from the Lord for me on the night that I was set free from the spirit if death, the words that I had taken to be my theme song, rung a chord with dynamic impact:

> *"Shake yourself from the dust, arise…"*

> Isaiah 52:2 (italics mine)

This was a type, not only of rising up from the shackles of demonic bondage, but the words now had literal meaning: I was to leave the dust of *Sanderstead* - all and that our home and the property meant to us; and we were to go on…….

When the disciples went to a town that did not accept their testimony, Jesus said they were to move on and *"shake off the dust from their feet"*, and I reckoned they should move on without tarrying.

Our search for another home was neither long nor complicated. Rob made us the offer of managing a delightful caravan park on the South Coast which belonged to an uncle of his. However, I asked Tim to turn this offer down, because there was no facility for keeping our horses in a suburban situation.

At about this time we met a missionary doctor and his wife, John and Pamela Fisher, precious saints, who ran a medical practice in a small village called Paddock about twenty five kilometres inland from Port Shepstone. The little village boasted the facilities of a farmer's hall, a police station, a post office and two or three Moslem owned stores. A factory had been built there in years gone by for the extraction of tannin from the bark of wattle trees. Evidence remained that, in its heyday, the business must have been a thriving industry. Considerable expense had been lavished on housing for the technical and professional personnel of the company. About a dozen solidly built old houses were set in a crescent in park-like surrounding some distance from the factory. With the advent of the formulation of synthetic tannin which went on to replace that extracted from wattle bark, it became no longer viable to operate the plant, and it thus closed down. The houses lay vacant for some years, and the place had become a ghost village. There were the remains of once beautiful gardens beneath mantles of overgrown weeds and creepers. Some fruit trees, citrus in particular survived the devastation of neglect over the years, and were still bearing fruit. This grand old establishment that had stood unwanted for so long was gradually being revived.

That is where John and Pamela set up their practice to offer medical treatment to the indigenous people, and to bring the gospel to them. They rented two houses in the complex, one in which they lived with their four young children, and the other was converted for use as a surgery. Another independent missionary family occupied one of the larger houses. One of houses on the far edge of the complex was run as a mission for homeless men.

The houses were situated a short walk from the school bus route, which meant that our children would not have to change schools. This was a big plus factor. However the deciding factor was the welcoming attitude and the love shown to us by the existing residents, most of whom were Christians. We were encouraged to join this community.

Tim and I were a little dubious about the condition of some of the vacant houses, but a certain house, nestling neglected beneath tall, spreading trees witnessed in our hearts as the place that God had for us. Not fifty metres from this house was a dilapidated row of garages, which were to become our horse stables.

*   *   *

A few days before Lucy's tenth birthday, which was on the third of March, a team of volunteers was present for the long distance ride to move the horses from *Sanderstead* to Paddock.

Our stable consisted of Lucy's pony Hotspur, Jill's pony Pebbles, Pauline's old show pony Rommel, Duhallow and Sika who had belonged to Lucy's best friend, Candice.

Sika was a Welsh-Arab cross, but the Arab in him prevailed, and he had reared with Candice, going over backwards, and she was terrified of him. Sika was a CA (children's A grade) show jumper. Lucy had the courage and the expertise to handle him, and thus Candice's father had given the pony to her. Lucy was delighted to have the beautiful dapple grey pony. Despite her background in riding, her natural ability and fearlessness, she had to use all her strength to control Sika and to match his cunning.

The first leg of the ride was from *Sanderstead* to my parent's sugar cane farm, about ten kilometres distant. The horses were to overnight there in the cattle kraal. Lucy rode the wayward Sika, and little Jill, who was eight and a half rode her beloved Pebbles on whom she always felt safe. A plucky, friend of Lucy's called Desiree, rode Hotspur, and another school friend of Lucy's called Phillipa rode Pauline's old show pony Rommel. I lead the convoy on Duhallow – a horse that always strove to be ahead. With the exception of Jill, who was much younger than the others, each child had a handful, particularly as some of them were not used to their mounts.

We took the ride slowly, and arrived a trifle breathless but safely at the highlands of my parent's farm. The farm, which was an extensive piece of land, rose steeply to a plateau above the Umzimkulu River. My sister, Pauline met us with much excitement, thinking back, no doubt, on the memories of her childhood, growing up with horses.

Pauline and I talked about the ride for the following day. We knew we would need an early start if we were to reach Paddock before nightfall. Either Pauline or I would ride Duhallow, and the one who was not riding would follow the convoy by car, excepting, of course on the tracks and bridle paths, when and if they could be found, to make the going more pleasant, at which times the motorist would stick to the highway.

The final plan was that Pauline would drive down the tar road leading to Port Shepstone, and then turn right just before the low level bridge to follow a sand track that wound along just above the river bank to a place at which we were due to rendezvous upstream from the Umzimkulu Sugar Mill.

I started off riding Duhallow, and all the children were up on their respective mounts. The first part of the ride through the farm was down an old road cut into steep slopes. The excavation serving as a road had not been maintained for countless years. Trees canopied overhead in the hairpin bends, and the air tingled with the aspect of the wild. We walked most of the way down, except for the odd pony which would jog now and then to catch up. The horses were alert to strange sounds and smells, and snorted occasionally in the early morning air.

When we reached the lowlands of the river bank, we found the sand road along which Pauline must have driven. One of the children even noticed tyre tracks on a part of the road where the sand was soft. We turned the horses right to trot along the level, wider, better track, which was a pleasant change to the overgrown, steep single pathway we had come down. As we followed the curves of the track the brown waters of the wide river could be seen on our left now and then when trees closer to the water did not obscure our view. At an open spot we could see in the distance the painted minarets of an Indian temple close to the water's edge on the opposite bank. I was thinking as I led our pack at a brisk trot: Tim had told me with delight of what wonderful people the Indians are when they are set free in the spirit. My husband liked people of all races; but he had a particularly soft spot for born again Indian believers.

Smoke from the boilers of the sugar mill billowed constantly upward, and could be seen on the skyline ahead of us to our left. The road narrowed and became rougher before a curve to the right; then, there in the distance the buildings of the Mill came into view upstream of the river. That was another thought: the Mill was the heart beat of the economy of our small town. When the international market could not absorb our sugar, or the floating rand in the international market adversely affected our currency so that other countries would not buy our sugar, bang went our small community! The Mill! The economy! The small business that was no longer viable! Our home!

I pulled Duhallow in, and called to the children to rein in likewise. There was a clearing ahead of us on the river bank, and in this clearing we saw Pauline waiting for us in the parked car. This place was a viewpoint from which we could look downstream at the Mill on the left, and upstream to where the river narrowed slightly and disappeared into the curve of steep hills. From this spot we could see the water marks made by the high and low tide levels against the steeper parts of the bank. This supported our knowledge of the fact that the river was tidal for some kilometres upstream from the sea. The tide was low as we cast our eyes around the vista before us. The river was, at a guess, between a hundred and a hundred and fifty metres wide at that place. We scanned the opposite bank with our eyes to find a cutting that would lead to a foot path diagonally upstream, maybe two to three hundred metres away. That cutting was the point to which we had to aim, and I explained this to Pauline and the children.

We knew that despite the low tide, the horses may have to swim at times. For this reason it was decided that Jill, who was the youngest and couldn't swim and Phillipa, who was the least experienced rider and seemed scared of the crossing, should travel in the car. Pauline and I changed roles. Instead of riding Duhallow, she rode her old pony Rommel. The reason for this was that although Duhallow was forward and on the bit under saddle, he was not a dominant horse of the herd, where-as Rommel was. Duhallow would follow, but Rommel probably would not. Jill's pony Pebbles was the sweetest most submissive of animals, both under saddle and in the herd. He was timid, didn't have the vestige of an independent spirit and would follow at all times, not wanting to be left out, or left alone. We put the stirrups up on the saddles of these two horses, and fixed the rein over their necks through the stirrups, but with ample give for them to stretch their necks.

Lucy, who was a bold rider on Sika, a very bold pony, set out over the wet sands to reach the water first. Desiree, who was also very plucky, but not as competent in the saddle, followed on Hotspur, remaining close on Sika's heels. Pauline, the only adult of the party brought up the rearguard on her honest old pony, Rommel. I sat comfortably in the car with the two younger children and watched the riders recede. The river bed was soft and sandy, and this made for easier going, as the horses did not have to pick their way between stones. The brown, muddy waters deepened as the party neared the centre of the river, but it was seldom deep enough to wet the riders feet in their stirrups. The party was taking the longer route across the diagonal to reach the cutting, but the two unmounted horses that lagged behind drifted slightly to the left of the riders, as this seemed a shorter line to the opposite bank.

They obviously reached a sandy ridge that ran lengthwise with the water, and I believed the worst was over as I saw the horses make good progress with water just up to their knees. Then I saw Lucy's horse almost stumble and start splashing as it went into deeper water. There was obviously a deep channel lining the far edge of the river which curved outward into the nook of our cutting. Sika was a strong pony and he seemed to bash the water furiously with his hooves, and then took some powerful strides to jump clear of the water, and leap up the steep bank ahead. Desiree took Hotspur through with courage and determination, and he soon leapt up the bank after Sika. Rommel followed a distance behind, and realizing the deep channel through which he would have to swim, seemed calm and unhurried in comparison.

Then I looked further downstream to see Jill's beloved Pebbles fall. He rose quickly, only to fall again, and send out huge ripples with the weight of his body crashing into the water. He kept on fighting, and was soon closer to the cutting, where he scrambled out. Duhallow was the last horse in the string. He had followed a path slightly downstream from Pebbles, who was already downstream from the riders. He slipped into the deep waters, and started to swim. Of a sudden I realized that he was not making progress. Instead of keeping his head well abreast of the water, which would be the case if his front legs were pawing water, his head was sinking into the water, and there was no splashing as of the pawing movement a horse makes when swimming......... And then we saw Duhallow go down further: his head was underwater; all that remained above the brown water was his muzzle pointing vertically upwards.

I presumed that Duhallow was caught in quicksand, and that the horse had given up hope, and was succumbing to drowning......... I panicked, and I was attacked by guilt and fear. I had chosen the route; I had chosen this spot to cross the river. It could have been one of the children that had gone down with their mount! Oh horror!

"Duhallow is drowning!" I cried.

Jill and Phillipa shivered, showing their distress.

I started praying in tongues, and to the children this was a most natural phenomenon. Then I turned and held their hands, and we prayed together in English, "Lord, save Duhallow."

Then while only a tiny vestige of Duhallow's chestnut fur below the smooth charcoal coloured skin of his nostrils could be seen, a black man came down the cutting, entered the water, took the horse by the bridle, and led him gently out and up the bank.........

"He's out! He's out!" came children's shouts from the back of the car as they jumped up and down in their seats.

This was South Africa, and it was to be expected to find a black man walking along a river bank in a remote part. I didn't think twice about where he came from or why he just happened to be there; without questioning I accepted his presence above the cutting at that time. With all my heart I was grateful that he was prepared to be helpful; and moreover that he was not scared of horses as many of them are.

However, we were eager to hear, from those present what had actually happened to save the horse from drowning.

When we met at the place we had chosen in a clearing where the cane lorries were loaded about a half kilometre above the river, Lucy was holding Duhallow, whom she had led, and Pauline was holding Pebbles, whom she had led from the river to the clearing.

Pauline called to us first as we came into earshot, "We nearly lost Duhallow!"

"Thank God for the African who pulled him out!" I said.

Lucy cried: "Mommy! Mommy! It was an angel who saved Duhallow. He suddenly appeared, as if from *nowhere*! I went immediately to thank him, and he was gone! Duhallow was caught in quicksand. So was Pebbles, but

Pebbles managed to get himself out as he crossed the river closer to us. That man just vanished. It was definitely an angel!"

I was thanking God that my child and her friend and my sister were not caught in the quicksand as well! What then? Praise God! They had crossed on a sound footing, and when the horses swam, they struck ground that was firm on the far side!

Then my logic prevailed: how could a normal human being pull a horse that weighs about four hundred kilograms out of quicksand with the rein of a mere bridle? We had seen so many broken bridles in our years of riding, and we knew that a bridle was never used in an instance where man had to pit his strength against a horse. A knowledgeable person would use a strong halter and rope. Given the circumstances no man pulling on a rope could pull a horse out of quicksand. And where did the human get his footing? The water was deep at that spot in the channel *God had sent an angel.* I knew that Lucy was not mistaken.

"Praise the Lord!" I cried.

We saddled the lead horses; the children mounted, and the band moved on towards Paddock.

NINETEEN

THE ARMIES WHICH WERE IN HEAVEN FOLLOWED HIM ON WHITE HORSES

A blessed time of the manifestation of God's provision followed. We were aware of the functioning of the body of Christ as never before. Several able bodied men from the mission cleared the property we arranged to rent, and assisted with essential renovations to the house. Melanie's husband, Dave Hampton sent his truck from Oribi to fetch our furniture and belongings. There were other deeds of Christian love that were too numerous to record. The families in the community showered us with love. Close bonds were formed between our children and children of the other families who lived there. Lucy, Jill and Sydney were swept up in the tide of good things the change had to offer, and adjusted to their new surroundings with joy. Lucy and Jill became the leaders of the horse riding squad. We had riding country at our feet that we had never dreamed of!

As we settled in to spend our first night in Paddock, Tim reached for a bible that was lying among an assortment of unpacked bags and boxes in our sitting room. He opened the book to II Corinthians, and read:

"For we know that if the earthly tent which is our house is torn down, we have a building from God, a house not made with hands, eternal in the heavens."

II Corinthians 5:1 NAS

That night we had a good, refreshing sleep, and we awoke to the smell of wood smoke – a delightful fragrance in our nostrils. Each house had an old fashioned wood fired boiler for the heating of the hot water supply. We found the new climate, and old fashioned heating facility exhilarating and exciting.

Tim reached an arm out to me as he awoke, and I snuggled closer to him.

"What a lovely tent, Charmy!" he cried.

I reiterated, "What a lovely tent........."

The house was considerably larger than the one we had left at *Sanderstead*, and the lounge looked very empty with our sparse furnishings. The house we had left also had fitted carpets, and the lack of a carpet in the new lounge emphasized the emptiness and dullness of the room.

The children had a great deal of exploring to do, and much of this was accomplished by running pell-mell with shouts of glee. Children from neighbouring houses also made early visits to us, the newcomers, and it was a delight to see them all as they ran hither and thither. Therefore, when Jill came running to me later in the day, I did not realize right away that she had come with important news:

"Mommy, Mommy, Mommy! Come, look, see!"

She dragged me from the unpacking I was busy with in one of the bedrooms. Her little hand was in mine as I followed her to the front door. She pointed outside, and my eyes met with the most incredible sight!

Rob and Dalene had arrived with a truck which was parked in our driveway. Rob had started supervising the offloading of furniture. Dalene and I ran toward one another, and embraced with loving hugs. I was breathless. The first item that Rob had taken off the truck was a beautiful, big, gold coloured carpet. He took this and placed it on the floor of our lounge!

"Praise God!" I cried. "Rob, what is happening?"

"The Lord is sending you some furniture with love in Jesus' name." He said.

Tim was helping with the offloading. He was smiling from ear to ear as he worked – not because of the things he was offloading, but because of the manifestation of God's provision. Every now and again he cried, "Halleluia!"

I noticed pieces of Rob and Dalene's upholstered brown lounge suite being assembled next to the old hydrangeas which grew between the house and the driveway.

I said, "Dalene, that's your lounge suite!"

"Yes it is. The Lord has shown us to go to the Cape. We can't take all our furniture with us, so we are bringing some to you."

"Glory!" I said. "I praise God for the furniture, but we will miss you so much!"

Tim and I were overwhelmed, crying alternately, "Praise God!" each time another much needed item came off the truck.

Soon the truck was offloaded except for one item – the heaviest of all.........
When, at last the men had taken it down, I recognized the *piece de resistance*: an automatic washing machine with a *spin dryer!*

There had been a time when I had cried.......... and God had heard my cry!"

A time of blessed fellowship followed with our dear mentors and beloved friends. Tim and I expressed our sincere gratitude, and listened eagerly as Rob and Dalene told us of their calling to the Cape.

* * *

Some days later while Tim and the children were out somewhere, Ruth, Emily and Frieda, the ladies who had been so good to me ministering deliverance, arrived with enough groceries to stock our larder for a fortnight. We stood in a circle holding hands and danced on the new golden carpet the Lord had given us, while I testified of His goodness. We were so happy and started singing praises to God as we danced. After a while we walked out on the verandah so my visitors could get a better look at the place.

Frieda couldn't get over the Citrus trees in full bearing, "Oranges and Lemons!" She cried, walking up to the trees.

Ruth looked across at the adjoining vacant plot. "And, are those horses I see? Are they your horses?" She queried pointedly.

"Our horses!" I said

"So many of them........." Frieda said. "Just when we'd got rid of a horse and his rider, now you go and get a whole lot more horses!"

Emily had her arm around me in a motherly fashion. I know that she was rejoicing on my behalf. Her smiling face was full of love.

"A whole lot more horses!" I repeated. "That one, over there, is Duhallow." I said pointing to the big chestnut. "The Lord gave me Duhallow. According to a vet, he had a terminal disease and would not live much longer. But he is very full of life nowadays, and can be difficult to control."

Emily tightened her grip on my shoulder, and I knew this to be a meaningful gesture, for she knew that the Lord had healed Duhallow.

"There was some drama when we brought the horses over here. Duhallow was sucked into quicksand when crossing the Umzimkulu. God sent an angel to pull him out!"

The ladies were wide eyed, and I heard intermittent cries of 'Halleluia' and 'Praise the Lord', and they asked me to relate the details of this miracle.

"Then there are Jill and Lucy's two ponies." I said, pointing them out. "The grey, grazing in the background is Sika. He's a wild thing, and threw his owner off, so he was given to Lucy. He's a top-grade children's show jumper. The other old brown horse is my sister Pauline's old show pony, Rommel That pony was notorious on the coast for collecting red rosettes. Pauline wants Jill to have him now. I also use him for riding lessons for the other children who live in this complex. Do you remember Peggy Maartens, whom I met at one of the bible studies? She brings her daughter out for riding lessons once a week. The riding has done a great deal for the child, who has to overcome fear, which is the result of an unstable home life and her father's tyrannical drinking. I have about half a dozen local little pupils. Many parents in this area have approached me to give lessons."

"Praise God." Ruth was saying, as we continued to walk on through the garden, inspecting what remained of the old flowers, shrubs and trees that had once been cultivated. This was once a beautiful garden!"

"Yes," I said, "It is obvious that no expense was spared in laying out the residences in fine, old, colonial style, judging by the architecture, the size of the gardens, and the type of plants that were established."

Frieda walked on round to the back of the house and found the old wood fired boiler made from a forty four gallon drum. "Well, really! If this isn't a relic of the past!"

"It makes very good hot water!" I exclaimed. "And the wood smoke smells delightful when one wakes up in the morning."

"Our God is so good the way He supplies all our needs." Emily exclaimed.

"Without even having to pay for electricity to heat the water – because the wood is plentiful around here." I finished her sentence.

We walked through the back door of the house into the kitchen, where I put a kettle on to the gas stove to make tea. The ladies helped me set a tray, and we carried it through to the lounge where we sat and relaxed.

Ruth said, "Do you know, talking about horses, I looked up scriptures about the *horse and his rider,* and I was surprised to find how many times it is mentioned in the bible.

"Yes, it is a term God uses to describe evil spirits, and powers of the air." Emily confirmed.

"I know! I know! I remember when Rob said those many months ago, 'a horse and rider is against you'."

Emily had her bible with her in a large hand bag, and she took it out to study some cross references: "In the day of the Lord, He promises to cut us off from the powers of darkness." She paged through her a well worn bible. "Here, in Psalms:

> 'At thy rebuke, O God of Jacob,
> both *rider and horse* were cast into a dead sleep.'

> Psalms 76:6 NAS

"And here, in Haggai is further evidence of the powers of darkness being overthrown in the day of the Lord:

'And I will overthrow the thrones of kingdoms, and destroy the power of the kingdoms of the nations; and I will overthrow the chariots and their riders, and *the horses and their riders* will go down, every one by the sword of another.'

Haggai 2:22 NAS

"This shows God's power over demonic sprits. Another threat to the horse and his rider is in Zechariah:

"'In that day, declares the Lord, I will strike every *horse* with bewilderment and his rider with madness. But I will watch over the house of Judah while I strike every *horse* of the peoples with blindness.'"

Zechariah 12:4

Ruth asked a question, as if to lead up to the answer she expected, much as a teacher would, "What weapon is God going to use to accomplish this purpose?"

Frieda jumped up, reached for the bible that Emily had been reading from, and stood paging earnestly through scriptures and cross references. Then, of a sudden, she started pirouetting on my gold carpet, hugging the bible to her breast as though she had something special that she was keeping from us. Eventually she calmed down and answered our expectant silence by saying,

"Let me read this scripture from Jeremiah:

'He says, you are my war club, My weapon of war;
And with you I shatter nations,
And with you I destroy kingdoms,
And with you I shatter *the horse and his rider.*"

Jeremiah 51:20-21 NAS

"Wow!" Several exclamations blended into one.

"Do you understand?" Ruth asked, and then went on to answer her own question: "God will use us, the believers, the house of Judah, to knock the enemy! It's dynamic!"

Emily said, "But here is another facet to the diamond. there are powers of darkness, but there are also powers of light….."

> 'For the Lord of Hosts will visit His flock,
> The house of Judah
> And will make them as *His royal horse in the battle.*"

> Zechariah 10:3 (italics mine)

Ruth took a bible off a nearby table and followed up from the same book:

> 'They shall be like mighty men,
> Who tread down their enemies
> In the mire of the streets in the battle.
> They shall fight, because the Lord is with them,
> And the *riders on the horses* shall be put to shame.'"

> Zechariah 10:5 (italics mine)

Emily augmented the subject: "Once again, confirming, the powers of light and darkness. I recall reading about the battle of Massada. It was a mountain fortress in which about a thousand of the remaining Jews took refuge, after the Roman massacre of Jerusalem about 70 AD. Before the Roman battering rams penetrated the last barricade to their stronghold, they gathered to hear the ancient sage. Words of wisdom in his address to them were: 'There are sons of darkness, and sons of light'. I have remembered those words I heard a long time ago, as they ring a special bell in my mind."

Ruth said, "I read in a legal document words to the effect, the masculine purports to include the feminine; therefore there are daughters of darkness…..."

Freida, chirped in with the interruption: "And we are daughters of light!"

"Indeed." Ruth finished.

I endeavoured to sum up: "We are weapons of God's warfare and God will make us like majestic horses in battle. This brings me to a thought from the book of Revelation. The message to the churches, is to *him that overcometh*….. Let's have a look at it:

> "And the number of the army of horsemen were two hundred thousand thousand: and I heard the number of them."

> Revelation 9:16 Authorised King James Version

Ruth again adopted her teacher's role: "Come on, who can do maths to work out that number?"

"Not me!" Frieda cried.

I found a pencil and some scrap paper and started writing down and counting noughts. "I get to two hundred million."

"That is confirmed in my New American Standard bible." Emily said. "These horsemen were commissioned to kill a third of mankind."

"The cavalry, no doubt are demon spirits." I said

"No doubt." Emily confirmed.

"Okay" I confirmed, "If there is a cavalry of demon spirits, then also there is a heavenly host of horse riders........."

"Yes!" Frieda was jubilant, "I have it here: Revelation nineteen, eleven:

> 'And I saw heaven opened; and behold a white horse; and he that sat upon him is called Faithful and True,; and in righteousness He judges and wages war.'"

Revelation 19:11 NAS

"I'll go on from verse thirteen:

> 'He is dressed in a robe dipped in blood; and His name is called The Word of God
>
> And the armies which are in heaven clothed in fine linen, white and clean, were following Him on white horses.
>
> And from His mouth comes a sharp sword, so that with it He may smite the nations; and He will rule them with a rod of iron; and He treads the winepress of the fierce wrath of God, the Almighty.
>
> And on His robe and on His thigh He has a name written,
>
> KING OF KINGS AND LORD OF LORDS.'"

Emily was reading ahead, and in a few words, summarized the facts in the last few verses of the chapter: "The scripture goes on to tell how the beast, and the false prophet, and those who have permitted the mark of the beast to be placed on them are overpowered:

'And the rest of them were killed with sword which proceeded from the mouth of Him who sat on the horse…..'"

Revelation 19:21

"Halleluia!" Frieda was standing up and boxing the air.

TWENTY

FOR I WILL RESTORE HEALTH TO YOU AND HEAL YOU OF YOUR WOUNDS

Those early days in Paddock were halcyon days: there was God's provision for our needs ministered to us by different Christians; there was the fellowship of the local Christians – the body of Christ – functioning and functional; there was the climate, which had the freshness and tang of a higher altitude; and there was the countryside a melange of sugar cane fields and forested areas.

If the days were halcyon days, the rides were a midsummer night's dream. The countryside stretching from the little village toward the renowned Oribi Gorge was marvellously scenic, and criss-crossed with pathways on soft ground. There was a narrow stream that meandered in great loops towards the Gorge to form one of the many breathtaking waterfalls of the panorama. When Duhallow knew we were approaching the stream he would snort and prance and begin to canter on the spot, straining to develop impulsion so that he could clear the stream with one powerful leap. When the cane fields are established a series of contoured roads are built in to enable the fields to be worked. These roads were a delight to ride on; and Duhallow knew that when the road was clear and could be seen curving uphill, it was the time to arch his neck and prance until he was let out into a full gallop. The cane roads were for brisk trots and gallops, but the forests were for the restfulness of a walk on a loose rein in the cool of the trees. On the edge of the pine and gum plantations there were, here and there, vestiges of the acacia forests that once covered the area. Riding in the forests was my favourite. I enjoyed the shade and the allure of the low light and the special atmosphere of the leafy covering overhead. In the forest there was expectancy, excitement, adventure. The acacia groves had left layers of twigs and leaves on the ground for decades, and this thick mat of decomposed and decomposing organic matter made a carpet that horse riders could only dream of. From the carpet underfoot, the captivating forest could be seen and felt: dark, gnarled tree trunks, wet with rain reached up to the abundant grey-green foliage comprised of myriads of compound leaves. The canopy above subdued the light. The cries of abundant bird life could be heard from the depths of the forest completing the mystery and enchantment of the scene. Who could embrace such romanticism in the most flamboyant art or architecture of the ages?

Duhallow was always alert in the forests. He would arch his neck and prick his ears forward, careful lest some strange creature dart out of the trees. I usually walked through the forests, not only lest some unexpected sight or sound made my horse shy, but in order to prolong the time spent in the cool shade and the beauty I so loved. I would breathe deeply of the fresh, moist air, as if to preserve the wonder of it all within me. God was doing a work of restoration. The forest rides were a type of pouring oil into the hurts of my soul – the inner healing that I needed. Here was a paradise in which I could find peace and joy; here was the fulfilment of the scripture in Hebrews:

> "There remains therefore a rest for the people of God. For he who entered His rest has himself also ceased from his works, as God did from His."

> Hebrews 4: 9,10

*   *   *

Paddock is situated 25 kilometres from Port Shepstone, the little coastal town where our studio was situated. Tim continued to try and keep our ailing business afloat. However, a characteristic phenomenon that always seemed to trigger the ignition of impending recession was the rise in the fuel price. The ripple effect of this was felt far and wide, and often tipped the balance between survival and the fall. The rise in the petrol price and the rise in the interest rate, engineered by fiscal policy, that cruel genie whose presence was unseen but whose influence was devastating, led to a malaise of social deprivation. Businesses closed. Jobs were lost. People feared.

Our business licences which were due on the first of January had not yet been paid; so we were trading illegally. Our rent was several months in arrears. There was actually no money to purchase film from the photographic wholesalers, as they marketed twelve-packs; so we had to buy one film per day from a retail outlet, in order to process the photographs at night and have them ready for the next day. Then, with the rise in the petrol price, we had to buy a litre or two at a time to keep going, and even the supply for this small quantity of the ugly liquid, dwindled as the days went by. And so, Tim closed down the studio.

I began to understand through reading and conversation that the recession was engineered by the International Monetary Fund and other big boys at the helm who were getting organized, and were not too concerned about the cost in terms of human discomfort. However Tim and I knew in the spirit that Jesus would make a way through the wilderness.........

Once we had settled in at Paddock and the decision had been made to close the business, which, somehow, just happened, without creditors proceeding against us, and without us having to file for bankruptcy, I asked, "What now, Lord?"

I received the answer simultaneously with the same inner nudge I had felt before when I had confirmed that it was the Holy Spirit that was speaking to me:

"Jeremiah thirty six, verse two."

I lost no time in looking up the scripture, which read:

> "*Take a scroll of a book and write on it all the words which I have spoken unto you* against Israel, against Judah, and against all the nations, *from the day I spoke to you,* from the days of Josiah, *even to this day.*"

"Praise God!" I cried. I knew exactly what the Lord meant. I was to write down all the things that He had spoken to me from that Monday morning in the darkroom, until this day – a period of just over half a year.

I started with an inadequate, old portable typewriter which could not even type all the letters of the alphabet, as some keys could not be depressed – but I knew the omissions could be filled in later. It was late summer, the month of March, the time when insects and flies multiplied to preserve the species through the coming winter. As I sat at a table with the rickety portable machine, I swept my arms left and right to disperse irritating flies on my arms, and I tied a cloth over the suppurating sinus on my right leg to prevent flies from landing there, for they were always drawn to the wound.

As the words slowly continued to be etched on paper, and the halcyon days progressed, a change occurred. I witness a marvellous miracle unfolding before my eyes: the nature of the flesh around the sinus in my right leg changed! The redness subsided, and granulation tissue began to form. After twenty years!

When I was sure that my eyes were not deceiving me, I called to Tim: "Timothy, look! Look! Look! The osteomyletis is healed! The wound is closing up!"

"Charmy! Praise God!" He cried. "Yes, I see. It's getting better. The wound is healing up!"

We waltzed on the golden carpet. Then the children joined us, and we held hands and danced in a circle on the carpet. Lucy, Jill and Sydney shared our joy, without even understanding why this exultation should be, and we sang the first lines of the gospel chours that Rob and Dalene had taught us:

> I could have danced for joy
> At such a wondrous thing
> Just to know that You are the King of Kings!

Tim said: "There were milestones in the healing process; but all the way we had to accept in the spirit that your leg was healed, without seeing a corresponding manifestation in the flesh. We had to look at Jesus, and not at the symptoms."

I said: "I understand God has commissioned me to write a testimony, and I have begun to tackle this as an act of obedience. Now, if I can explain, as I proceeded with the manuscript I noticed a change coming in the colour and texture of the scar tissue. Praise the Lord. It is so exciting!"

Tim's arm was around my shoulders, and he said: "I remember Rob's telling us, 'the kingdom of heaven is righteousness and peace and joy in the Holy Spirit.'* Today, we have entered into the kingdom of heaven by faith.

*Romans 14:17

EPILOGUE

"In this Year of Jubilee each of you shall return to his ancestral property."

Leviticus 25:13

A trumpet is sounded in the land as it is the year of jubilee. Two thousand and fourteen is the year which this book goes to print. Tim and I have been married fifty years; and we are able to return to our possession.

God opened doors supernaturally in the years that followed our stay in Paddock.

Recently, Tim and I holidayed in Margate. On the way home, he expressed a desire to visit our old property at Sanderstead. There was a surprise awaiting us . . .

We found the entrance to the servitude road that led to the property canopied beneath mature Macadamia Nut trees, and as we came out of the trees, we saw a high pitched roof where our house, which had had a slightly pitched roof, stood. Approaching closer, we saw green, mowed lawns, shrubs and tall trees set in park-like array. The picture was one of grandeur, beauty and peace. We were met at the gate by a friendly lady, who asked us in.

The lady and her husband, who is an artist, gladly gave Tim and I a tour of the buildings and surrounds. The house and garden had the presence, elegance and proportion of a manor house. Here and there we were able to see part of an original wall that we built, but the building had been so cleverly and artistically added to, that little of the original floor plan was recognizable. There was an entrance hall, and a series of reception rooms in split levels; there were chandeliers, alcoves featuring sculptures, and walls hung with original art. Four en-suite bedrooms were offset from spacious living rooms. A dining room with selected artworks led to a functional, attractive kitchen. Ferns hung from pots in brass holders, and ceramics of bright colours were displayed on the shelves of a wooden divider between the two rooms.

Our hosts, the owners of the property, invited us to coffee on the terrace, from where we could see the sea, enjoy the sunshine and view the Cycads and other exotic garden plants.

Tim asked, "What do you do about water?"

"We have a borehole in the valley, which has never run dry. It yields five thousand litres per hour." Our host replied.

The evidence of water was all around! We told them of our struggle with rain water tanks that ran dry in some seasons.

"Did you do the building alterations?" I asked.

A poignant story was about to unfold . . .

"No. It was he previous owner!" He mentioned the name - the name of a famous South African artist.

I repeated the name with astonishment, for I knew that name well! That name had had an uncanny significance to me at a time, some years previously, when my daughter, Jill, told me she was corresponding with an artist's daughter who wanted to buy a horse from her, but the child never reached the point of getting her parents to finalize the deal.

"My daughter had been in touch, time and again, with his little daughter who was about twelve or thirteen years old. The child desperately wanted a horse." I could witness the longing in the heart of a little girl who wanted a horse – all the more fervently because there was an undercurrent of financial trouble in the family.

"There were money problems . . ." our host sighed.

"I gathered that, and so did my daughter. In the end Jill ministered the horse to the child. Little did she know that it would come to this very property!"

"He did all these building alterations! It is sad. They had to move from here . . ." Our host continued.

"Indeed, the architecture is the work of artist!" Tim said.

"What vision he had!" I commented.

"Yes, they moved to the southern Cape. Unfortunately he died there."

"I am sorry!" Tim and I echoed in unison.

Our host continued: "The property is in the market again."

He mentioned a price that I knew was insufficient to cover the cost of drilling and equipping the invaluable borehole, plus doing the renovations and extensions to the house, in terms of the real value of money at this time . . .

On our drive home, Tim said "It the completion of a full circle in our lives."

We knew that we had been blessed sufficiently to repossesses the land. There was an ethereal realm in which I visualized an aureole of iridescent colours in the wake of our orbital path . . .

In recording this testimony, I trust that I have put emphasis where emphasis should go; and that I have illustrated and brought into focus facts that have been blurred in the background of the religious and economic mosaic of our age. When heaven opens, and Christ appears riding on a white horse, I trust that you and I will be riding with Him, mounted on white horses – and that we will be numbered among the troops of heaven following Him on white horses.